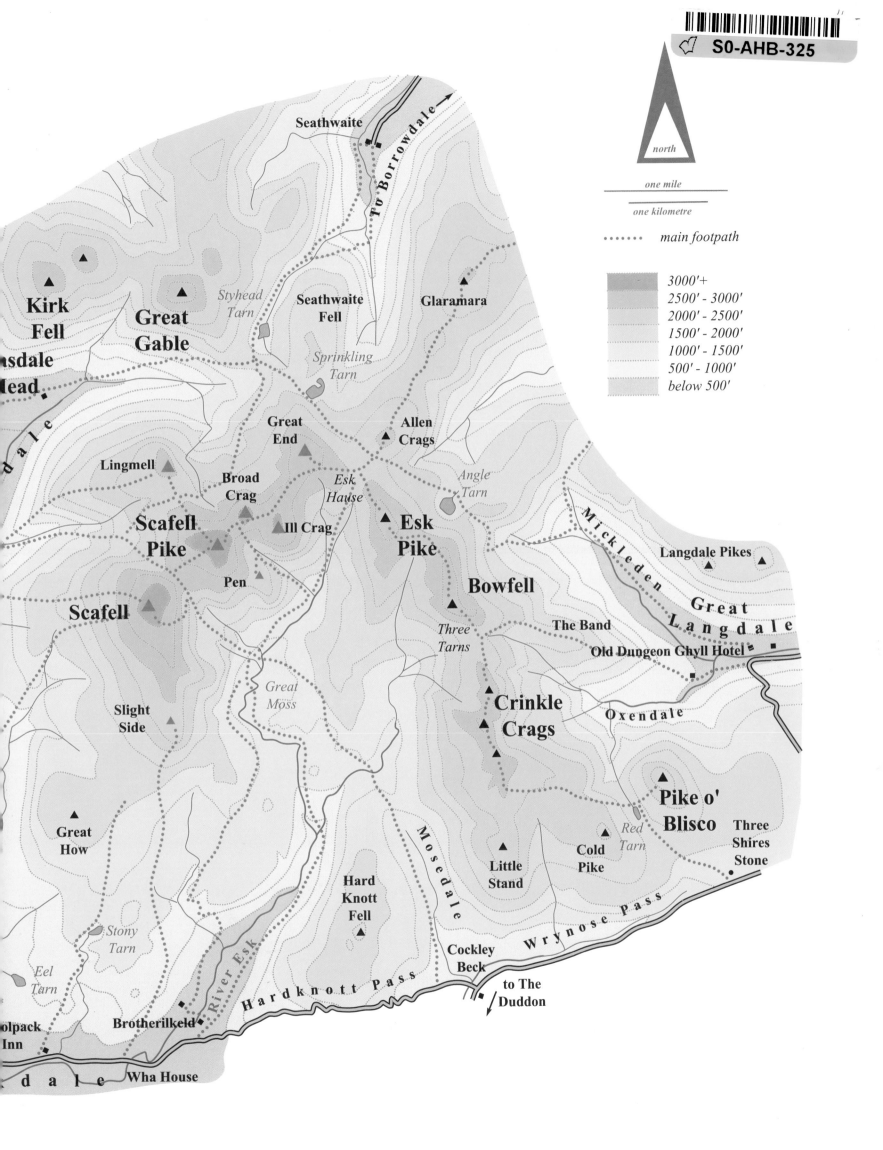

SO-AHB-325

north

one mile

one kilometre

············ main footpath

3000'+
2500' - 3000'
2000' - 2500'
1500' - 2000'
1000' - 1500'
500' - 1000'
below 500'

Seathwaite

To Borrowdale

Kirk Fell

Great Gable

Styhead Tarn

Seathwaite Fell

Glaramara

Sprinkling Tarn

nsdale Head

dale

Lingmell

Great End

Allen Crags

Broad Crag

Esk Hause

Angle Tarn

Scafell Pike

Ill Crag

Esk Pike

Mickleden

Langdale Pikes

Pen

Bowfell

Great Langdale

Scafell

The Band

Old Dungeon Ghyll Hotel

Three Tarns

Great Moss

Crinkle Crags

Oxendale

Slight Side

Pike o' Blisco

Great How

Little Stand

Red Tarn

Three Shires Stone

Cold Pike

Stony Tarn

Hard Knott Fell

Mosedale

Eel Tarn

Cockley Beck

Wrynose Pass

River Esk

Hardknott Pass

to The Duddon

olpack Inn

Brotherilkeld

dale

Wha House

SCAFELL

Portrait of a Mountain

FRANCES LINCOLN

SCAFELL

Portrait of a Mountain

Bill Birkett

This book is for all those who love mountains and wild, unspoilt places

Acknowledgements
So many people have helped in the preparation of this book that it is impossible to detail them all. To all those missing, the many friends and climbing companions with whom I've shared days on the Scafell, my apologies. To the many that keep reading my books, enjoy my imagery, talk to me on the fells, send me informative emails and letters, thanks: your opinions and knowledge are of great value to me.

A special thanks to my family for their forbearance: Sue my wife (particularly for first draft editing), Rowan my daughter, William my son. A number of people checked various parts of the book: for checking the historical sections my particular thanks to John Adams, Peter Fleming, Colin Read, Andrew Sheehan and Jeremy Sheehan. For use of archive photographic material: Abraham Photographic, John Adams, Colin Read and Al Phizacklea. For local knowledge and assisting me with the photography: Jill Aldersley, Dave Birkett, Colin Downer, Pete Fleming (for the loan of his wonderful Scafell Pike stone axe), Rick Graham, the Harrisons of Brotherilkeld Farm, Mary Jenner, Maureen Penman, Sue Vickers, George Sharp, Luke Steer.

Thanks to Jackie Fay, Librarian at Kendal Mountaineering Reference Library; Jane Renouf at Ambleside Library; all at Cumbria County Council Libraries, and also James Archer, Grevel Lindop, Jamie Lund, Jamie Quartermaine and Ronald Turnbull for invaluable assistance with research.

To Anquet Mapping for supplying me with their excellent computer map information, the Lake District 1:25,000 Explorer Maps all on one CD which runs seamlessly. To Martin Bagness for drawing the maps.

To John Nicoll of Frances Lincoln who encouraged me to take on this project and has faith enough to publish my work. To Jane Havell who, in difficult circumstances, took on the massive volume of material I supplied her with and shaped it into this special book.

To those protective bodies and groups who care about the Lake District and seek to protect its unique character and beauty: the National Trust, the National Park Authority, the Countryside Commission, English Heritage and the Friends of the Lake District. May they retain 'their eyes to see and hearts to perceive'.

Bill Birkett Photo Library
Bill Birkett has an extensive photographic library covering all of Britain's mountains and wild places including one of the most comprehensive collections of photographs of the English Lake District. For photographic commissions, information, prints or library images, telephone 015394 37420, mobile 07789 304949, or email bill.birkett1@btopenworld.com. Web address www.billbirkett.co.uk includes regularly updated images.

HALF-TITLE: In the wilds of upper Eskdale, beneath the gaze of the Scafells, a climber approaches Great Moss en route to the mighty Esk Buttress (locally called Dow Crag). It is early spring: rock climbing on this magnificent buttress is feasible early and late in the year, despite its high location, due to its south-facing aspect.

TITLE PAGE: Nearing the head of Wast Water, the view over the lake opens to the heart of the Scafells and the hanging corrie of Hollow Stones. The cliffs of Shamrock and Scafell Crag stand to the right and Pikes Crag to the left. George Sansom (of Central Buttress fame) thought Wasdale the finest mountain valley in the whole of Britain.

CONTENTS

OPPOSITE: Looking along the edge of Great Moss to the Esk Buttress (in cloud shadow), with the triangular top of Pen perched on top.

INTRODUCTION

Mountains: earth set a little higher, a greater view, a wider horizon. Remote from the hurly-burly of everyday life, they have huge appeal. Some visitors are drawn by their poetic beauty, their ethereal ever-changing light and form, their mysticism, intrigue or history. Others find fascination in their unique flora and fauna, or in the complex rock structures that have made them. Some like their isolation, purity of air and independence of spirit. A few seek to take on their challenge by climbing the steepest crags or running the most demanding terrain while at the same time dealing with extremes of mountain weather. The vast majority enjoy walking among the hills, experiencing nature at its most fundamental, finding satisfaction in topping the recognised high points or enjoying breathtaking views to distant peaks. In truth, it is a magical mix of many qualities that places mountains at the centre of many people's lives.

What gives a mountain a real character is difficult to define. Nakedness and impressiveness of form, steep challenging heights, altitude, changing weather patterns, the surrounding environment – these are just a small part of the myriad characteristics that shape how we feel about an individual mountain. Beauty is in the eye of the beholder, and all mountains are unique.

This book is about the Scafells, the highest and most powerful group of mountains in England. It portrays the whole mountain Massif – from Great End to Slight Side, via the Pikes of Scafell and Scafell Mountain – throughout the seasons, in many different moods and from many vantage points. The photographs were taken between, sometimes during, the climbs I have done and the trips I have made. My aim is to portray the distinctive beauty, drama and sheer power of the Massif, while also capturing some of its most special features.

Glimpsed from afar, from valley base or ideally from neighbouring heights, the Scafells present an alluring and sublime skyline, appearing as an impressive wave of naked piled rock, sharp ridge and steep crag which soars high above shadow-filled hanging coves and deep valleys. Detailed acquaintance serves only to enhance this impression. Rise to these heights and you walk the roof of England. Explore them further and you discover great steeps and precipices which have captivated and challenged climbers and mountaineers for some two hundred years.

***

There are many facets to the attractions of these mountains: the scream of the peregrine falcon as it flashes from its nest across the face of Cam Spout Crag; the bobbing sea of cotton grass spread across the wastes of Great Moss; the neck-craning, dizzy heights of Scafell Crags; the East Buttress or the sentinel bastion of the Esk Buttress to set the climber's pulse racing; or, with feet in the clouds and a high position, the rewarding views across the surrounding fells of Pillar Mountain, Great Gable, Bowfell, Harter Fell, Dow Crag and distant Black Combe. For those who love wild beauty, these hills have much to offer. For members of the climbing fraternity who take up the challenge and adventure of the heights and steep places, it is nothing less than hallowed ground.

At its heart can be found the highest point of the whole Massif, the great domed summit of Scafell Pike. Stand on this point and the view north-eastwards over the heights of Broad Crag and Ill Crag, along the extended spine to Great End, reveals an undulating sea of stony desolation. Only the rock islands of the tops themselves protrude through the pile of broken scree. Originally these tops were referred to collectively as 'the Pikes of Scafell'; Scafell Pike itself was only so named when it was confirmed by the original Ordnance Survey of 1860 to be the highest point of the whole Massif.

Turn and look to the south-west and even more dramatic mountain scenery is revealed. Here, beyond the deep gap bridged by the knife-edge arête of Mickledore, lies the great bastion of what was once known as 'Scafell Mountain' – before the early surveys, this was thought to be the highest point. Isolated from the rest of the Massif, it is guarded by huge cliffs either side of Mickledore: Scafell Crags above Wasdale and the East Buttress above Eskdale. The direction of the Massif now turns south over the rocky top of Scafell to fall in a long ridge down to Slight Side. This twist in the tail presents Scafell in stark relief and gigantic elevation compared with the rest of the group.

During the last Ice Age the volcanic heights of the Scafells occupied the highest point beneath the overlying ice. From this hub the glaciers flowed to gouge out the deep distinctive dales of the region. When the ice finally melted, it left the rock-strewn heights of the Massif standing high above the valleys of Wasdale, Borrowdale, Langdale and Eskdale, all of which radiate outwards like the spokes of a wheel. These corridors now form the main routes of approach, from which most people form their first impressions of the Massif.

Judging by the Neolithic axe factory on the south-western slopes of Scafell Pike and the abundant stone shelters around the heights, the delights of the Massif have been enjoyed since earliest times. The Norsemen gave it the name Scau Fjall, which is still reflected in the local pronunciation

'Sca-fal', whereas the popular pronounciation is 'Scaw Fell'; it means stony or rocky hill. Since those times, shepherds have run their sheep across its extensive, if somewhat bare, heights. They must have known it well, built some of the ancient marker cairns, and taken most of the paths and ways that are widely used today.

After the publication of early guidebooks to the region, interest in the scenery of the Lake District grew steadily, boosted by the influence of the Romantic poets. On a long ramble around the region in 1802, Samuel Taylor Coleridge ascended Scafell and descended by the steeps of Broad Stand. This takes a line of hanging shelves and corners through the crags above Mickledore, the ground dropping steeply away beneath. Although it had probably been used by local shepherds and mountain men for centuries, it is steep and potentially perilous, requiring the use of both hands and feet.

From the summit of Scafell, Coleridge wrote to the love of his life, Sara Hutchinson, of his daring exploits: 'surely the first Letter ever written from the top of Sca' Fell!'

O my God! What enormous Mountains these are close by me, & yet below the Hill I stand on / Great Gavel, Kirk Fell, Green Crag, & behind the Pillar, then the Steeple, then the Hay Cock – on the other side & behind me, Great End, Esk Carse (Hause), Bow-fell & close to my back two huge Pyramids, nearly as high as Sca' Fell itself, & indeed parts & parts of Sca' Fell known far and near by these names the hither one of Broad Crag, and the next to it but divided from it by a low Ridge Doe Crag.

William Wordsworth's *Guide to the Lakes*, published in 1810, became a bestseller.

Soon, however, all had changed. Polite interest from those who could afford the luxury of travel gave way to a frenzy with the arrival of the railways which, for the first time, opened the region to the less privileged classes. Leading the march was the Kendal and Windermere Railway Company, with the construction of Windermere station in 1847. The West Coast Whitehaven and Furness line was also completed in 1847, providing access to the remote dales, deep lakes and high mountains of Wasdale and Ennerdale. With the completion of stations at Coniston in 1859 and Keswick in 1865, rail access opened all doors to the Scafells and the incoming tourists took to them with a relish. All routes to the heights were explored and many travelled on foot, recording what they believed to be original paths. Some were even carried by pony from Wasdale, Langdale and Borrowdale to within a short distance of the summit of Scafell Pike.

Despite the pronouncement of Auld Will Ritson, first innkeeper of what is now the Wasdale Head Inn, that 'nowt but a fleein' thing could git up', one of the first recorded rock climbs was made on the East Buttress of Scafell, via Mickledore Chimney, in 1869. The Keswick-based Abraham brothers, mountain photographers and climbers, commenced their work of record in the 1880s and continued for over half a century. Their beautiful imagery of dales and steep places and their fine mountaineering books proved an enormous influence. In a relatively short space of time, many were to discover the delights of the Scafells.

TOPOGRAPHY

The Scafells are comprised of a continuous and unbroken mantle of stone and boulder, a landscape of primeval power likened by Dorothy Wordsworth to skeletons or bones of the earth not needed at the creation. At an altitude hovering around 914m, they run initially in a south-westerly direction from Great End, the north-easterly head of the Massif, to the highest point, Scafell Pike, located at the centre. Stretching for some 2km, this section takes the form of a broad undulating ridge, flanked by Ill Crag at the southern edge of the plateau and Broad Crag to the north. A natural route of passage leads along the line of intersection, descending and ascending the gaps between the high rocky domes of Great End, Ill Crag, Broad Crag and Scafell Pike. From the heights, these 'Pikes of Scafell' take on the appearance of separate rocky islands which have somehow collided to remain fused together. Below lie rocky steeps, hanging coves, deep gills and great runs of scree. Either side of the Massif flanking Scafell Pike are the outlying tops of Lingmell, above Wasdale, and Pen, above Eskdale. But this is only half the story.

Beyond Scafell Pike the Massif drops some 150m into the gap of Mickledore, only to rise again, above the most awesome horseshoe of cliffs in England, to the summit of Scafell. Scafell is the most impressive bastion of the whole Massif, and for a long time it was thought to be the highest point; to the naked eye, the rocky knoll on its summit, whether viewed from near or far, still can appear to be so. The direction of the mountain now turns south to fall in a long rough ridge down Long Green and over the buttress atop Cam Spout ridge to Slight Side. Beyond Slight Side the heights rapidly diminish, first to Eskdale Fell and finally into Eskdale.

The bulk of Great End is the most familiar aspect of the Scafells when viewed from the valleys of Langdale or Borrowdale. Its considerable north-east face gazes down Grains Gill towards Seathwaite; when plastered in snow, it appears both massive and formidable. Its angled pitch, for the most part slightly less than vertical, and its relatively high altitude means that it holds the snow more than any other part of the Massif; as a result, it is the most popular winter climbing cliff in the region.

BELOW: Looking from the valley floor, over Seathwaite Bridge, first to Seathwaite Fell and then to Great End, the north-eastern final terminus of the Scafell Massif. The midsummer greens of the valley contrast with the bare rocky high tops.

ABOVE: Sprinkling Tarn is one
of the highest and most
charismatic tarns among the
Lakeland fells. It has recently
been stocked with the rare
vendance from Bassenthwaite
in an attempt to preserve the
species: I wonder how the
resident brown trout feel about
the intrusion?

Nestling beneath its north-west foot lies Styhead, the high point of the pass between Wasdale and Borrowdale, and, a little closer to the cliff itself, the waters of Sprinkling Tarn, one of the most beguiling of the region. Below, to the south-east, the high shoulder of Esk Hause links routes to Borrowdale, Eskdale and Langdale: reputedly this is England's highest crossroads. A famous cross-walled shelter stands here, providing protection whichever way the wind may blow. Above Esk Hause, the path skirts the flanks of Great End to rise through Calf Cove, the last watering hole before the crest of the Massif is gained. There is a further cross-walled shelter here, and lush grazing before the stony desert. Iron rings sunk into nearby boulders indicate where ponies were once secured; from this point onwards, only Shanks's pony could take you to the summit of Scafell Pike.

A broad shoulder leads over to the south and the twin rocky tops of Ill Crag; its more substantial westerly top is generally regarded as its summit. The crest leads to the col beneath Broad Crag, and a north-easterly view to the magnificent Wasdale face of Great Gable. Ascent to the upper reaches of Broad Crag, somewhat narrower than Ill Crag, leads to a main path following a level, bouldery plateau beneath the rocky knoll of the summit. Relatively few make the extra effort to scramble to the very top of Broad Crag, because the scene ahead is dominated by the mighty summit

dome of Scafell Pike, the highest point of the whole Massif.

Before reaching this, a steep rocky descent must be made to the bare col that forms the head of both Piers Gill, falling north to Wasdale, and the steep scree of Little Narrowcove, falling south to Upper Eskdale. A very steep ascent then continues until the dome begins to level out. The raised cairn at the summit – a circular stone construction with steps leading to a platform – constitutes the highest point in England. The trig point stands just a little lower, to the northwest of the cairn.

Although the dome dips rapidly to the west, with paths descending towards Lingmell and Mickledore, to the south and east the level plateau extends to the knoll of the Eskdale cairn. This marks the top of the ridge that sweeps down over Pen and the Esk Buttress to the Great Moss of Upper Eskdale, and east by numerous circular stone shelters to a curious little walled, now roofless, building, complete with stone hearth, side benches and flagged floor. The structure is probably early Victorian, built at the same time as the cross-walled shelters, the iron pony rings and the grand summit cairn: it might have been built by the early surveyors, or as a tea house to offer refreshment to the many tourists by then flocking to the summit.

On the ridge below the Eskdale cairn, beneath Rough Crag, little Pen is considered to be an independent top. It occupies an airy position with Ill Crag opposite, looking over the depths of Little Narrowcove and the wildness of upper Eskdale's Great Moss stretched below. The terminus of the ridge is formed by the great rock sentinel of Esk Buttress: a clean pillar of some 107m of vertical rhyolite, one of the most beautiful and striking climbing crags of the region. Esk Buttress is the climbers' name; local farmers call it Dow Crag and it is also marked on maps as Central Pillar.

From Scafell Pike's trig point, the main route falls initially north-west down through featureless boulder fields towards Lingmell col, with the route to Mickledore veering off in a south-westerly direction after 100m. Although cairned, Lingmell col is easy to miss in the mist. Beyond, the ground rises to the rocky knoll summit of Lingmell itself. The isolated Lingmell Fell is a fine and dramatic mountain, occupying a commanding position above Wasdale Head with outstanding views to Scafell Crag, Kirkfell, Gable and Pillar and down the length of Wast Water. Its position, nestling below England's highest mountain, means that it remains relatively quiet and untrod.

The way leading to Mickledore, over boulder and stone, is not particularly well defined, and the path bifurcates in places. North-west of the path lie the steeps of Pikes Crag (marked as Pulpit Rock on Ordnance Survey maps), and around 200m south-east the tiny Broadcrag Tarn (altitude 830m). This, along with Fox's Tarn (altitude 826m) in the hanging cove south of Scafell's East Buttress, is not so much a tarn as a tarnlet.

Mickledore itself takes the form of a short, sharp ridge, grassy near the top on the Eskdale side before turning to steep scree, but immediately rocky with steep scree streaming down on the Wasdale side. It effectively joins the boulder-strewn heights of Scafell Pike with the awesome cliffs of Scafell. On the Scafell Pike end rests a Mountain Rescue Box, holding stretcher and first aid equipment, while the Scafell end abuts a steep rock barrier. In summer, climbers leave their rucksacks on the sunny Eskdale side,

seek shelter from any prevailing westerlies, and eat their sandwiches here, resting between climbs.

For walkers, there is no safe way on to Scafell directly from Mickledore. For scramblers and climbers, the stepped corners of the infamous Broad Stand start through a fissure between a huge block and the solid crag a little way down the Eskdale side. The first recorded descent was made by Coleridge in 1802, and the first recorded ascent by Messrs Ottley and Birkett in 1815. This was the passage that the famous fell-walker Alfred Wainwright never made. Who could blame him, for the ground tumbles rapidly away at this point and even the first ledge beyond the fissure is tremendously exposed. This is no place to make a slip.

No map can do justice to the power and size of the cirque of Scafell's cliffs arrayed either side of Mickledore. They are easily the most formidable and impressive in the whole of England. Climbs here include the most famous and challenging in the country, and the intriguing story of their climbing portrays the essence of British climbing history.

Sweeping in a great arc leftwards from Mickledore are the cliffs of the East Buttress. Their profile is that of an overhanging, bulging barrel-side: water dripping from the face of the crag here lands a frighteningly long way away from its foot. Not until the corrie holding Fox's Tarn is reached does the angle ease, and the route by this tarn offers the easiest ascent of Scafell from Eskdale or Mickledore.

Extending right from Mickledore, overlooking the high cove above Hollow Stones, are the complexities of the Scafell Crags whose dominant character is stunning verticality. Working across the face from the left, Botterill's Slab defines Central Buttress before the independent towers of Pisgah and the Pinnacle are followed by the huge rent of Deep Ghyll. To the right of this stands the final high crag, Deep Ghyll Buttress. At this point, separating the buttress above from the steep and complicated crags which plunge down to Shamrock and Hollow Stones, a natural fault known as Lord's Rake leads up and across the face. Walking routes up Scafell from this side include Lord's Rake (with a potentially dangerous balanced block atop the first rise) and the West Wall Traverse, which doubles back from Lord's Rake beneath the balanced block, to enter and finish up Deep Ghyll.

Once atop the crags, tempting though the nearby summit may be, the rock outcrop of Deep Ghyll Buttress (labelled Symonds Knott on the Ordnance Survey map) is well worth the climb. Its reward a stunning view down to Wast Water, it could be considered an independent top in its own right (although at the time of writing it was not classified as such in my Complete Lakeland Fells). In the col beyond Deep Ghyll Buttress is a stone cross laid out on the ground. Useful in poor visibility, it points north-west to the head of the Green How descent to Wasdale, north-east to Deep Ghyll and so to the West Wall Traverse and the base of Scafell Pinnacle, south-east to Fox's Tarn and to the Eskdale path, and south-west to the summit of Scafell.

A cairn on a rock outcrop and a ruined shelter, which repeatedly changes shape as people add and subtract to its construction, mark the top. The view from Scafell includes fells far and near, Burnmoor Tarn and Eskdale and all of Will Ritson's seven kingdoms. As he told the bewildered Bishop of

LEFT: A Rescue Box, complete with stretcher and items of first aid, is strategically situated on the ridge of Mickledore. Principally, the Scafells are served by the Wasdale Mountain Rescue Team. It is purely a voluntary organisaton, with around forty dedicated team members who also have full-time jobs, and is dependent on voluntary donations. Founded in the early 1970s, the team deals with around sixty incidents a year.

OPPOSITE: From broad bases some 100m below, it is quite astonishing that the Pinnacle (left) and Pisgah (right) end as free-standing twin towers at the top of Scafell Crag. Warning: don't stand here if you haven't a good head for heights!

Carlisle in about 1860: 'Why, there's England, Scotland, Wales, Ireland, the Isle of Man and, you of all people should know this, Bishop, there's Heaven above and Hell below.'

With superb views to Bowfell, the Crinkle Crags and over Harter Fell, the rocky shoulder falls then levels across Long Green to make a little ascent to the buttress that tops the ridge leading down to Cam Spout Crag. The South Ridge of Scafell continues to fall to the rock outcrop of Slight Side, the last and neatest top in the Scafell Massif. Beyond lies Eskdale Fell and, finally, lovely Eskdale.

GEOLOGY

The igneous rocks from which the Scafell Massif is built were produced by volcanic eruptions at the end of the Ordovician period some 440 million years ago. The molten rocks, spewed out of the top in the form of ash and volcanic bombs, flowed down the sides as lavas and protruded through the crust beneath in the form of dykes and plugs. Differing rocks, with varied properties and degrees of hardness, are made of hard, fine-grained, flinty ashes known as tuffs at one end of the spectrum, and lavas of rhyolite and andesite at the other. These in turn are interspersed with mineralised intrusions and faults, filled with breccias and weaker materials.

The rocks thus formed are collectively known as the Borrowdale Volcanics. Under subsequent periods of erosion, their variable hardness has produced the rugged topography and irregular knobbly slopes, the rocky summits and great rock faces that are so distinctive of this range. Following the volcanic eruptions came the Tertiary Period, when the whole central mass was lifted to form an elongated dome. Drainage of water from the high point, the Scafells, cut through the rocks to define the distinctive wheel-spoke structure and the radiating valleys which form the Lake District.

Successive periods of glaciations followed, in what is known as the Quaternary Period. These were spread over 150,000 years or so, with the last receding a mere 11,500 years past. The ice, flowing from the highest points – separating Scafell Pike from Scafell – deepened the valleys, carved out the high coves and vertical crags, and scooped out the depressions that became the tarns and lakes. Protruding from the ice, the summit rocks were shattered by the sub-zero temperatures. Below these, snow and ice peeled the bedrock clean, piling masses of boulders and scree down the slopes.

A fine-grained andesite tuff running through the Pikes of Scafell, similar to that found in the Langdale Pikes, was used in Neolithic times, c. 5,000–2,000 BC, to produce stone axes. Though not as extensive as the Langdale axe factories, a number of sites have been worked, most notably on the western slopes of the summit dome of Scafell Pike. Along the heights of the Scafells, mineralisation has occurred to a lesser extent than around the radiating valleys and, to my knowledge, no mineral mines or slate quarries are to be found within the high Massif. However, small garnets are embedded in the rocks around Esk Buttress, as well as lower down in Grains Gill. In mineralised faults below the Esk Buttress and Scafell Crag's Lord's Rake, there are samples of fluorspar.

SOIL AND CLIMATE

Many events have shaped conditions on the Scafells. Since the last ice age, weather conditions have fluctuated; acidic rocks have broken down to produce nutrient-rich soils, and primary habitats of summit, heath, bog and flush (deposited material washed out by rain) have been established. The varied use of the land has also made its contribution, from early farming and tree clearances in Neolithic times to more extensive grazing in the Viking era, on to intensive farming and over-grazing in the present day, combined with the growth of tourism and leisure use.

A rain gauge sited at Sprinkling Tarn, a significant distance from the much wetter summits, has consistently recorded a mean annual rainfall of around 4700mm. This reveals the Scafells, along with Snowdon in Wales and the Knoydart Hills in the Western Highlands of Scotland, to be among the wettest places in Britain. Significantly, however, the nature of this wetness is more favourable than in other regions – seriously! The rain over the Scafells tends to fall thick and heavy, producing sudden deluges with extensive dry periods between, rather than lingering as a fine mist or cloud for protracted periods. High summer can bring sudden thunderstorms; climbing on the East Buttress, I have experienced lightning striking the crag with explosive force – not an experience I would wish on anyone!

Of course, weather conditions increase markedly in severity with altitude. While it may appear relatively warm in the valleys, conditions can feel arctic along the tops. Generally, even discounting the considerable wind chill factor, temperatures drop by one degree centigrade for every rise of 150 metres. The summit of the mountain is therefore some six degrees centigrade colder than the valleys below. Even if it feels mild in the car park, the steeps of Scafell can be frozen hard.

BELOW: A tiny red garnet in a broken rock by the path below the East Buttress. Grains Gill above Borrowdale is the location most noted by geologists looking for garnets, but in fact they are widespread throughout the Scafells.

BOTTOM: A lump of green fluorspar from the mineralised vein that runs beneath the East Buttress. If you shine an ultra-violet light on it, in dark conditions it fluoresces in a very dramatic way. Due to oxidation of impurities within the fluorspar, however, the lustre and colour of this rock will rapidly deteriorate. Unusually for the Lakeland fells, the Scafells have escaped the scars of mineral mining and quarrying.

Snow cover and longevity are intermittent here. Warm fronts from the Atlantic can quickly bring rain to reduce blanket snow cover to patchwork, or even strip it altogether. Even with climate change, there may be exceptional winters when snow and ice lie thick and unbroken for months at a time. On the high tops snowfall before the end of October is usual, and the Massif frequently turns completely white even before the end of September. The coldest month tends to be February; although there may be little to no snowfall then, the heights may be mantled with ice. I have experienced late blizzards in March, occasionally in April and even in May. Though in no way comparable to the heights of Ben Nevis or the Cairngorms where snow may linger all year round, the north-facing heights and gullies of Great End and Scafell Crags can hold snow into the summer.

Frequent winds are a characteristic of the oceanic climate, with the western seaboard receiving the brunt. Scafell is the first stop for these winds after the nearby coastline, and the high tops take a severe blasting during southwesterly gales, which are prevalent and most violent during autumn and winter. On the heights of the Scafells, winds can average over 100 mph with gusts of up to 150 mph.

Naturally, this fell is often shrouded in cloud; on average, the cloudbase around Wasdale is lower than anywhere else in the Lake District. Additionally, the mere physical presence of the mountain can shield large areas from sunshine. In winter, when days are short and the sun is low in the sky, many north- and north-east-facing slopes stay in shadow. This means lower temperatures, as well as the risk that sodden and saturated areas may never dry out.

FLORA

Despite the extreme pressures of climate, sheep and people on the plant life of the Scafells, it is remarkably varied and rich. Markedly affected by altitude, soils and meteorological conditions, there are five different classes of plant habitat. These are the apparently bare rocky 'summits', combined with cliffs, ledges and deep gills; the areas of 'flush', where springs burst forth carrying soils and nutrients; the 'bogs' of stagnating water, bearing plants with the ability to generate their own nutrients; the 'heaths', which form the upper limits of sheep pasture, and the 'watercourses and tarns'.

Colonisation of this landscape by plants has been an ever-changing evolution since the end of the last ice age. Initially, an arctic-alpine flora thrived, though this changed with the prevailing climate, the evolution of soils and the liberation of nutrients from the eroding rocks, as well as with the effects of man. Amazingly, many of the arctic-alpine species hold on, notably the purple saxifrage found in the sheltered and protective recesses of Piers Gill.

While the stony tops may appear barren and bare, there is life to be found in the form of club mosses and lichens, with dwarf willow and juniper sheltering among the boulders. Depending on the season and prevailing weather conditions, lichens can give the rocks a most spectacular colour, particularly around Scafell Pike where sometimes they appear to glow scarlet. This phenomenon was described by Dorothy Wordsworth and included in later editions of William Wordsworth's *Guide to the Lakes*, under 'Excursions to the top of Scawfell and on the banks of Ullswater':

I ought to have mentioned that round the top of Scawfell-Pike not a blade of grass is to be seen. Cushions or tufts of moss, parched and brown, appear between the huge blocks and stones that lie in heaps on all sides to a great distance, like skeletons or bones of the earth not needed at the creation, and there left to be covered with never-dying lichens, which the clouds and dews nourish; and adorn with colours of vivid and exquisite beauty. Flowers, the most brilliant feathers, and even gems, scarcely surpass in colouring some of those masses of stone, which no human eye behold, except the shepherd or traveller be led thither by curiosity: and how seldom must this happen!

It is a remarkable observation for a once-only visit: I wonder how many people walk through these same boulders today without even noticing the lichens?

Another sighting to be made on the high rocky ledges between April and October is sea pink or thrift. This beautiful and brightly coloured flower occurs on the coast and in the mountains because it can tolerate the harsh conditions experienced in both localities. Once the plant was known locally as 'Scafell pink', and it was not until pioneering botanist James Backhouse confirmed it to be sea pink in the 1860s that it was accepted as the same species.

Flushes, at the emergence of springs, can provide little areas of plant life – there are numerous examples on Scafell, typically at Calf Cove above Esk Hause, and Hollow Stones below Scafell Crags. Where water comes to the surface after percolating through nutrient-rich rock, it can provide habitats for mosses and liverworts, and flowers such as starry saxifrage and yellow mountain saxifrage.

Bogs provide a home for a variety of plant life; Great Moss, nestling below the Esk Buttress in Upper Eskdale, is a typical example. They generate their own nutrients and have been encouraged by wetter and cooler climatic conditions. Slowly expanding since the Bronze Age, they have encroached on the uplands, overwhelming birch and alder woods – the skeletons of these trees can often be seen in the peats that the bogs have deposited. In summer, great seas of

ABOVE: Widespread over the rocks of Scafell Pike – and particularly noticeable on the regular path descending from the summit to Mickledore – are rocks that appear to be scarlet. In misty or damp conditions, the coloration is particularly intense, almost fluorescent. This is not a geological phenomenon, but due to the presence of a certain lichen.

cotton grass swaying in the wind are the most obvious plants, though close inspection reveals cross-leaved heath, crowberry, bog asphodel and the spiky red-tipped hairs around the folding leaves of the insect-eating sundew.

Beneath the heights, the heath habitat extends at the limit of useful sheep grazing; the heights around Burnmoor Tarn are typical. Here are the three heathers, bell, ling and cross-leaved, as well as the berries of bilberry, bearberry and juniper. Tarns and becks also provide a further habitat for a considerable variety of plants – a brief splash of richness and colour before the frosts and snows of winter return again.

FAUNA

The high Massif of the Scafells does not support a great variety of bird life, since few British birds nest in the cold montane zone above 600m. The golden eagle, ptarmigan and elusive dotterel, birds of the high mountains, are thought to have bred here during the 1700s but had gone by 1800. Interestingly, they disappeared before the advent of mass tourism and the upsurge in climbing and hill walking. The golden eagle did make a comeback of sorts, nesting during the 1960s and into the early 1970s; at the time of writing, however, it has disappeared once more.

Some magnificent birds have permanent residence here, though, while others return to breed during the spring and summer. Among the former, the great black raven has a full clutch of eggs by mid March when it can still be decidedly chilly; lining its nest of sticks with sheep's wool helps combat the cold. The raven feeds on carrion, the most prevalent being sheep. The peregrine falcon also breeds here; seen diving in a stoop on its prey of small to medium sized birds, it is an awesome sight. Like the raven, it nests on steep, inaccessible crags which abound in the Scafells, laying its eggs about a month later.

In winter, looking like a squally shower of snowflakes, flights of snow buntings arrive from northern climes to feed around the stony summits. But spring is the time for most of the birds to return. The wheatear's appearance in late March is the first sign that the spring migration is under way in the mountains and uplands. With its distinctive white tail bar, perky bobbing stance and cheerful burst of song, it is a most welcome sight. The ring ouzel, a bit like a blackbird in appearance but with a distinctive white collar, the meadow pipit and the skylark follow.

The fox is the most celebrated indigenous animal. Local legend tells of the 'old grey fox', reputedly greyer in colour and much bigger than the red fox of today. Foxes breed in borrans, large piles of hollow boulders which provide subterranean refuge and are well scattered beneath the crags throughout the region. They compete with ravens for carrion and also eat the short-tailed vole, one of the few other animals that lives in these hills. They are still hunted by the Eskdale and Ennerdale Foxhounds, despite the anti-hunting legislation of 2005. Stoats also seem to operate to an altitude of around 600m, although they do not turn white in winter as is common in the Highlands of Scotland. Frogs, another food source for the higher predators, are also frequently found to an altitude of 600m.

On spring and summer evenings, brown trout can be seen jumping for flies on the high tarns of Burnmoor, Styhead and Sprinkling Tarn. During 2006, the rare vendance, a herring-like fish said to be a remnant of the last ice age, appeared in Sprinkling Tarn. Formerly found only in Bassenthwaite or Derwent Water, 134,000 vendance eggs were transplanted by RAF helicopter at the behest of the Environment Agency because of failing stocks in the two large lakes, thought to be caused by increased silting and pollution. Following a similar logic, perhaps we may one day see the brown bear and wolf return to these rugged tops!

Many common butterflies find their way to the lower flanks of the Scafells, typically the Meadow Brown, Small Tortoiseshell and Small Heath. By far the rarest and most interesting is the Mountain Ringlet – deep velvet brown, with a band of orange blotches towards the edges of each slender wing. It flies for a few weeks only, between the end of June and mid July. Colonies are found to an altitude of 1000m, but emerge from the mat grass only when the sun shines, when the butterflies can be seen sunning themselves by slowly fluttering just above the ground. Scafell Pike also provides a home for the montane beetle, *Nebria nivalis*.

ABOVE: Ravens, the most common of the large, high-mountain birds, are early nesters and can be with chick in March. They eat only carrion and do not kill other species to survive. They love to show off and will often give impressive impromptu aerial displays.

ABOVE: The remains of a Peregrine kill below Cam Spout Crag. Peregrine falcons are ruthless predators diving in a stoop at up to 240 mph. They can work as a pair, male and female, with one bird driving a flight of pigeons or similar smaller birds while the other flies in from a different direction to intercept the prey. When they have made a kill, the tiercel (the male bird) usually plucks the carcass and prepares it for the hungry young. This is done at selected sites known as 'plucking points', which are often littered with the victims' feathers. The tiercel then flies high and calls the hen from the nest. She flies beneath the tiercel, turning upside down at exactly the right moment to grasp the kill in her talons as the tiercel drops it, in a matchless display of split-second timing and precision teamwork.

OPPOSITE: A midsummer view north over Upper Eskdale from the flanks of Harter Fell. The trees mark the line of the River Esk, with Taw House Farm on the left and Brotherilkeld on the right. Beyond lies the Scafell Massif to the left and Esk Pike to the right.

Since the last ice age retreated, some 11,000 years ago, there has been a remarkable history of human involvement with the rocky heights of the Scafells, beginning in prehistory at least 7,000 years ago with Neolithic man manufacturing stone axes near the summit of Scafell Pike. This important interaction between man and mountain has continued to this day, peaking over the last two centuries with the upsurge in tourism and massive interest in walking and climbing.

Scafell Pike, along with the Langdale Pikes, was a major centre for stone axe production during the Neolithic period and extensive workings and chipping sites remain. It is interesting that both centres for axe production have the common name 'Pikes'. On both sites, the raw material, a fine-grained andesite tuff known as Seathwaite Fell Tuff, was roughed out and a basic stone axe produced by chipping the rock with a tougher rock known as a hammerstone. It is thought that axes were roughed out on both sites over thousands of years. They played a hugely important role in changing the face of Britain, enabling stone-age man to fell the trees that were then dominant on the lower heights and in the valleys. These axes were the tools that empowered man to change his role from opportunistic hunter-gatherer to that of organised farmer. They have been found throughout Britain and Europe.

Below the heights, there are many remnants of the Bronze Age. Undoubtedly the most striking around the Scafell Massif are the extensive remains on Burnmoor. Here there are many piles of stones, which could be either hut circles or burial mounds, and five distinct stone circles. The most prominent of the circles is known as Brat's Hill, formed by forty or more stones arranged at an average diameter of 30.5m. Even more striking are Sampson's Stones, on the edge of Great Moss near the source of the River Esk. This array of boulders is presumably natural, as they are so huge that it must surely have taken the force of nature to shift them; other bumps and collections of boulders in the area are smaller.

Coleridge commented on Sampson's Stones on his descent from Scafell to Eskdale in 1802:

Just at the bottom of the Hill I saw on before me in the Vale, lying just above the River on the side of a Hill, one, two, three, four Objects, I could not distinguish whether Peat-hovels, or hovel-shaped Stones – I thought in my mind, that 3 of them would turn out to be stones – but that the fourth was certainly a Hovel. I went on toward them, crossing and recrossing the Becks & the River & found that they were all huge stones – the one nearest the Beck which I had determined to be really a Hovel, retained its likeness when I was close beside / in size it is nearly equal to the famous Bowder stone, but in every other respect greatly superior to it – it has a complete Roof, & that perfectly *thatched* with weeds, & Heath, & Mountain-Ash Bushes . . .

Pollen analysis from Burnmoor Tarn suggests that forest clearance on the moor started c. 2000 BC; it is presumed that stone circles and early farming began shortly after this, around the middle of the early Bronze Age. The sites of axe manufacture around the tops are commonly thought to be of early Neolithic origin, although carbon dating of the peat–chippings interface near Pike o'Stickle in the Langdale Pikes suggested, to huge surprise, that axe manufacture could date back to Mesolithic times, c. 6000 BC. Further tests are yet to be done to verify this, but if the early date was confirmed it would be very exciting news.

All in all, the Scafells are home to a rich prehistoric landscape of great importance in Europe. Owing to the relative remoteness of the region and the fact that it was of little economic importance in mining or quarrying or to modern intensive farming practices, the summit rocks have been little disturbed for literally thousands of years. They are like an open book, just waiting to be read. However, with the upsurge in hill usage, particularly among walkers, this situation could change all too quickly. Already the summit area of Scafell Pike has become a dispiriting mixture of the old and the new, with 'outdoor groups' constructing rough shelters from what appears to the uninformed eye to be simply an endless pile of rock. However, this 'random' pile of rock contains a considerable archaeological and historical legacy. Provided they are left undisturbed, ruined ancient structures, walls, piles of stone, excavated hollows and the like may one day reveal a fascinating tale of man's involvement with this amazing landscape over aeons of time.

One of the best views of the Scafells is from the Roman fort on Hardknott Pass, above Brotherilkeld, at the head of Lower Eskdale. I wonder if, looking out from their fort building, soldiering and administrating, these Roman visitors were tempted to scale the heights? It would be hard to imagine they were not. Or did the Celts of the Iron Age make the heights their last stronghold? On the Eskdale side is a considerable track which climbs by Scale Gill and traverses through the delightful corridor by Silverybield Crag to Great

OPPOSITE: One of the stones in Brat's Hill stone circle, looking out to the summit of Scafell. This is the largest and most complete of five stone circles high on Burnmoor, above Boot and below Scafell. Constructed from Eskdale's red-and-white granite, they are thought to date from the Bronze Age, about four thousand years ago.

Moss. Is this Roman? Did they extract peat here to burn, or did they build the track to keep an eye on the inhabitants of Great Moss? Maybe the track dates from a much later period of history. Who built the long, straight, stone walls in Great Moss, now ruined and cut through by the meanders of the young River Esk – Celts, Romans, Vikings, or the Furness monks from Brotherilkeld? Whose are those matching walls and structures atop Scafell Pike? And I wonder if the Vikings signalled from the rocky heights of their 'Scau Fjall' (stony mountain) to the not so distant and similar-sounding 'Snae-fell' (snow mountain) on the Isle of Man.

The mountain is traversed by a network of packhorse tracks taking the easiest route from one valley to another. Esk Hause, the highest mountain pass and crossroads in England, forms the centre point. From here a route leads on to the summit spine itself, or down to each of the surrounding valleys: Wasdale, Borrowdale, Langdale, Duddon and Eskdale. Allegedly, it was the Romans who brought the ancestors of the Lakeland fell pony to these shores. Is that when this form of transport and movement of goods began? In the 1100s, the monks of Furness Abbey wrote their ledgers with wad (pencil lead) from the graphite mines of Seathwaite in Borrowdale – were they frequent users of Esk Hause?

THE BEGINNINGS OF TOURISM

The sublime nature of the Lake District mountains, lakes and dales was firmly established in public consciousness during the 1700s. Fr West, a Jesuit priest posted to Dalton-in-Furness, published a best-selling guidebook to the Lake District in 1778. He wrote:

> Particularly the taste for [painting] – induces many to visit the Lakes – there to contemplate in Alpine scenery, finished in nature's highest tints, the pastoral and rural landscape – the soft, the rude, the romantic and the sublime of which perhaps like instance can no where be found assembled in so small a tract of country.

He recommended some 21 viewing stations from where he thought the best views of the Lakes could be enjoyed. Rather pedestrian, perhaps, though it was a start. With more of an eye to the heights, William Wilberforce – parliamentarian, leader of the campaign against the slave trade, co-founder of the Royal Society for the Prevention of Cruelty to Animals (RSPCA) – recorded in his book of 1779, *Journey to the Lake District from Cambridge*, being shown in Cumberland 'a high hill with a kind of crack in it – said by the People thereabouts to be higher than Skiddaw'. This was

ABOVE: Early morning on the upper reaches of the River Esk, and a great pool of shadow spilling across Great Moss dramatically reveals the true size of the crag of Esk Buttress at more than 90m. The rugged skyline is topped by Scafell Pike standing centrally, with Ill Crag to its right. Surprisingly, out of this stillness, I heard the voice of a climber on the East Buttress, instantly recognisable. It was Dave Birkett (who else?) making the film Set in Stone *(see page 174); he and his team had been at the crag since sunrise and I had no idea he was going to be there!*

the Scafells, and the crack was the gap of Mickledore dividing Scafell Pike from Scafell 'Mountain'.

Ornithologists noted in the 1700s that the golden eagle, ptarmigan and dotterel inhabited the tops of the Scafells. Yet by the 1800s, even before mass tourism took off and rock walking and climbing began, these high mountain birds were gone. A combination of factors was probably responsible for the decline: early egg collecting, the keeping of nearby moors for grouse shooting, and climate change. Within Britain these birds are now to be found only in the Highlands of Scotland.

Samuel Taylor Coleridge, along with the other Romantic poets who based themselves in the Lake District in that creative period heralding the beginning of the nineteenth century, certainly made his literary mark. Unlike his contemporaries, he also made history by physical action as well as by metaphysical supposition. The recorded modern history of Scafell begins with his mind-blowing descent of what is now known as Broad Stand on 5 August 1802. This natural line of weakness, a series of rocky steps and corners, climbs from Mickledore through the craggy steeps to find the shoulder of Scafell above the great cliff of the East Buttress on the Eskdale side, and Scafell Crag on the Wasdale side. On the steepest section near the bottom, Coleridge descended by the simple expedient of hanging from his hands and dropping to the next ledge below. He was completely ignorant of what was to come, and entirely incapable of climbing back up. Nothing had ever been written about this route prior to Coleridge's account; inspired by him, the first recorded ascent – the very first rock climb made on the Scafells – was achieved in 1815. Today, rock climbers use it as an easy way down between the crags, although most fell runners and

walkers find it too difficult to tackle without a rope or safeguarded by a climber. Coleridge descended in ignorance, accepted that he could not retrace his steps and that he was out of control, breaking all the rules of safe mountaineering, but his was nevertheless a breathtaking, inspirational and audacious achievement.

His letter to Sara Hutchinson, written the next day at what is now Taws Farm in Eskdale, is surely one of the most gripping passages in mountain literature, arguably equalled only by Joe Simpson's relatively recent *Touching the Void*:

> I slipped down, & went on for a while with tolerable ease – but now I came to a smooth perpendicular Rock about 7 feet high – this was nothing – I put my hands on the Ledge, and dropped down / in a few yards came such another / I *dropped* that too / and yet another . . . but the stretching of the muscle of my hands & arms, & the jolt of the Fall on my Feet, put my whole Limbs in a *Tremble*, and I paused, & looking down, saw that I had little else to encounter but a succession of these little Precipices . . . – So I began to suspect that I ought not to go on / but then unfortunately tho' I could with ease drop down a smooth Rock 7 feet high, I could not *climb* it / so go on I must / and on I went / the next three drops were not half a Foot, at least not a foot more than my own height / but every Drop increased the Palsy of my Limbs – I shook all over, Heaven knows without the least influence of Fear / and now I had only two more to drop down / to return was impossible – but of these two the first was tremendous / it was twice my own height, & the Ledge at the bottom was [so] exceedingly narrow, that if I dropt down upon it I must of

RIGHT: Broad Stand, with a figure attempting the longest, steepest corner where Coleridge hung from his fingers before dropping to the ledge below.

necessity have fallen backwards & of course killed myself. My Limbs were all in a tremble – I lay upon my Back to rest myself, & was beginning according to my Custom to laugh at myself for a Madman, when the sight of the Crags above me on each side, & the impetuous Clouds just over them, posting so luridly & so rapidly northward, overawed me / I lay in a state of almost prophetic Trance & Delight – & blessed God aloud, for the powers of Reason & the Will, which remaining no Danger can overpower us! O God, I exclaimed aloud – how calm, how blessed am I now / I know not how to proceed, how to return / but I am calm & fearless & confident / if this Reality were a Dream, if I were asleep, what agonies had I suffered! What screams!

Finally, on the last ledge, comes the conclusive evidence that this was indeed Broad Stand. He wrote:

I glanced my eye to my left, & observed that the Rock was rent from top to bottom – I measured the breadth of the Rent, and found that there was no danger of my being wedged in / so I put my Knap-sack round to my side, & slipped down as between two walls, without any danger or difficulty –

Other important influences that brought about increased interest in Scafell included William Wordsworth's bestseller, *Guide to the Lakes*, first published in 1810. Later editions included a section entitled 'Excursions to the top of Scawfell', but it is doubtful whether William ever got to the summit; the account, although not credited as such, was in fact written by his sister Dorothy, who visited the summit in 1818 with her friend Elizabeth Barker who lived at Newton Place, opposite the Borrowdale Hotel. It must have been a perfect day, for Dorothy recorded in her journal: 'There was not a breath of air to stir even the papers which we spread out containing our food . . . and the stillness seemed to be not of this world.'

Two guidebooks from this era began to detail not just the dales and lakes but also the high fells. The first was William Green's guide in two volumes of 1818–19, with the all-encompassing title *The Tourist's New Guide, containing A Description of the Lakes, Mountains, and Scenery in Cumberland, Westmorland, and Lancashire, with some Account of their Bordering Towns And Villages*. A subtitle continued: *Being the Result of Observations made during a Residence of Eighteen Years in Ambleside and Keswick*. Maybe the title was not so catchy as Wordsworth's, but this was a sterling work, part guide and part travelogue, which not only detailed the fells but reported on first-hand exploration, including the first ascent of Broad Stand. Green, a Manchester surveyor and a fine artist with a prolific output of engravings and drawings, had settled in Ambleside in 1800 and was undoubtedly a remarkable character.

Jonathan Otley's guide, *A Concise Description of the English Lakes*, followed in 1823, with numerous subsequent updated editions. Although based on a trigonometrical survey by Colonel Mudge of c. 1800, it was Otley who unequivocally defined Scafell Pike as the highest point of the Massif and the highest mountain in England. He wrote:

The lower of these points, lying to the south-west, is a bulky mountain – the proper Scawfell; the higher rising from a narrower base, has been called the Pikes. For want of a designation sufficiently explicit, strangers have sometimes been mistakenly directed to the secondary point; and to cross the deep chasm of Mickle Door, by which they are separated, is a work of considerable difficulty; although the direct distance does not exceed three quarters of a mile. Latterly however, it seems by common consent, the highest point is called Scawfell-Pikes; and since the erection of a large pile and staff upon it in 1826, there is no danger of mistaking the place.

Otley was well placed to note that reaching 'Scawfell' by way of 'Mickle Door' was a 'work of considerable difficulty', for it was he, guided by Edward Birkett, who had made the first ascent in 1815. Otley, a clockmaker from Keswick, had taken to exploring the district in his spare time. Fascinated both by its natural history and especially its geology, he was the first to describe the three great rock groups of the Lake District, and helped his fellow Cumbrian Adam Sedgwick, Professor of Geology at Cambridge, to determine and understand the region's principal geological features.

Naturally, once identified and recorded as the highest top of the greatest mountain Massif in England, Scafell Pike became a considerable attraction. As is the case today, many were drawn to climb it and its appeal generated a sizeable tourist trade. A coach and horses would have been the principal mode of transport for those arriving in the valleys of Langdale, Borrowdale, Eskdale and Wasdale. From the heads of these valleys, those disinclined to walk rode ponies on well-established packhorse tracks to the highest point of the mountain they could practically reach. In Calf Cove above Esk Hause, the highest mountain pass in England connecting all routes from the valleys, the iron rings once used to tether the ponies remain set in the rocks. Calf Cove was the obvious stopping point: beyond this, the going becomes rough and bouldery; the cove with its natural spring and lush meadow was an ideal place to rest, graze and water the ponies before they made their steep return back to the depths of the valleys.

The distinctive cairn on the summit of Scafell Pike was erected in 1826, and the cross-walled stone shelters on Esk Hause and in Calf Cove at around the same time. These

OPPOSITE: The cross-walled shelter on Esk Hause, probably constructed in the Victorian era to cater for the upsurge in tourism; an identical one is to be found in Calf Cove. They offer some kind of shelter from the wind, but are not too great when it rains!

OPPOSITE, BELOW: Calf Cove, below Great End, is traversed by the main paths from both Borrowdale and Langdale. This was the last watering and grazing point before the path rises to the rocky spine of the Massif. In Victorian and Edwardian times, tourists carried on ponies from Borrowdale, Wasdale and even distant Great Langdale had to dismount here.

LEFT: One of a number of iron rings sunk into the rocks of Calf Cove, through which ponies were tethered while visitors continued on foot to the summit of Scafell Pike.

simple, open wind shelters are quite ingenious, providing shelter whatever the direction of the prevailing wind. Similar ones are found elsewhere on the high Lake District fells, notably on the summit of Helvellyn. Along with the summit cairn, other structures, now ruined, once provided shelter. The most remarkable, reasonably intact though now roofless, stands a hundred metres or so east of the summit cairn. With four walls, an entrance in the side and a fireplace at the far end, it has a flagged floor and benches of stone. It was probably a tea house, and it must have done a roaring trade. There are similar structures on the high mountains of Snowdonia; served by mountain railway, the Snowdon café remains operational to this day. E. Lyon Linton, in *The Lake Country*, published in 1864 two years after the Ordnance Survey, refers to a roofless structure near the summit of Scafell Pike as the 'Ordnance Survey Shelter'.

When the railways arrived in the late 1840s it became a great deal easier to visit the region. Up to this point, with the exception of a few enlightened locals, exploring the

beautiful Lake District, particularly the high fells, had been open only to the privileged classes – the cost of travel and accommodation, and having the luxury of sufficient free time in which to indulge these activites, precluded all but a lucky few. The Kendal and Windermere Railway Company and the West Coast Whitehaven and Furness line both began in 1847; stations were built at Coniston in 1859 and at Keswick in 1865. With the railways came power for the working man to leave the city behind at the weekend:

So I'll walk where I will over mountain and hill
And I'll lie where the bracken is deep;
I belong to the mountains, the clear running fountains
Where the grey rocks rise rugged and steep.
I have seen the white hare in the valleys
And the curlew fly high overhead,
And sooner than part from the mountains
I think I would rather be dead.

Chorus
I'm a rambler, I'm a rambler from Manchester way,
I get all my pleasure the hard moorland way.
I may be a wage slave on Monday,
But I am a free man on Sunday.

Ewan McColl, 'Manchester Rambler'

Because of its very nature, slogging across the fell-sides on foot, fox hunting has always been open to all classes in the Lake District. For many it was much more than a sport: it was the freedom of the fells and a glorious release from the six days' toil necessary for every working man to feed his family. At first, hunting took place with individuals collecting together *ad hoc* to set off to find the fox. However, in 1857, at the foot of the Scafells, a character called Tommy Dobson formed the first official pack of foxhounds in the region – the Eskdale and Ennerdale hunt. To the locals of the area, Tommy Dobson was a much loved and revered figure. Any hounds seen roaming the Scafells will most probably be descended from this pack. The Lake District boasts a proliferation of songs, still sung at the annual shepherds' meets, that tell of the thrill of being out in the mountains and the camaraderie of hunting:

I'll tell you a cure
For a malady sure,
A cure that goes straight to the heart
It's the sound of a horn on a fine huntin' morn
Who could wish for anything more
It turneth the grave into gay
And makes pain into pleasure give way
It makes the old become young and the young
    become strong
So let's go a-huntin' today.

Tommy Birkett, 'Hunting Day'

This was also a remarkable period for the furtherance of science and the understanding of the natural history of the high fells. Botany in the area took a large stride when Hewett C. Watson, 'the father of plant geography', came to the Lake District in 1833. In his wake followed a series of Victorian botanists who were to make new finds and records. Active on the fells were a group of Quaker botanists, notably two James Backhouses, father and son. In the 1860s they found alpine hawkweed on the Scafell range, and confirmed that the beautiful plant known locally as Scafell pink, an orb of pink flowers suspended on a long narrow stem in flower between April and October, was the same as the sea pink found along the coast and in mountain areas.

When the Ordnance Survey published the first detailed map of the Scafell Massif in 1862, a huge advance was made in understanding and navigating through the region. Along with the growing walking fraternity and the 'peak baggers' already inhabiting the fells in increasing numbers, the first exploratory rock climbers began to make their mark. From this period until the turn of the century, momentum grew in the climbing fraternity. Mountaineering saw a shift of emphasis from the Alps to the British crags, helped by an increasing awareness of the challenges to be found on the great faces of Scotland's Ben Nevis, Wales's Snowdon and Lakeland's Scafell. Larger-than-life characters came to the fore, none larger nor with greater impact that O. G. Jones, who claimed that his initials stood for 'Only Genuine' (his forenames were in fact Owen Glynne). A London schoolmaster of Welsh descent, he was revealed to be a bold climber of great skill and incredible strength. His Lakeland mentors, offering local knowledge, inspiration and encouragement, were the Keswick-based photographers, the Abraham brothers.

The influence of the Abrahams was profound; to this day it is almost impossible to open a book about early mountaineering without seeing their imagery, nor to enter a climbing inn without seeing their photographs on the wall. And their work touched a much wider sphere than the mountaineering fraternity, contributing to a particular public perception of the rugged beauty of the Lakes. The three brothers, George, Ashley and John, operated from their photographic

LEFT: The brothers Ashley and George Abraham, photographed in the 1930s.

ABOVE: Owen Glynne Jones, one of the finest and most daring pioneers on Scafell Crag, killed in 1899 in the Swiss Alps. Jones's book Rock Climbing In The English Lake District, *first published in 1897, was one of the most influential works ever published on rock climbing.*

ABOVE RIGHT: The entrance to the Wasdale Head Inn, Easter 1895, strewn with climbing ropes and boots.

shop in Keswick. George and Ashley were also known as the Keswick Brothers, a name given to one of their climbs put up in 1897 on the flank of Scafell Crag. They carried between them a plate camera of mahogany and brass which had to be mounted on an equally sturdy tripod. To get the camera to location, it was broken into sections which were distributed among the brothers and at least one assistant. Ashley became the first president of the Fell and Rock Climbing Club formed in 1906, and George was elected an Honorary Member of the Alpine Club in 1954. They were also great fans of early motorised transport.

Much activity now began to be centered on the Wasdale Head Inn, conveniently nestling at the foot of Scafell, which became the undisputed Mecca for climbers. Tales from this period are legendary. George Abraham wrote of O. G. Jones who, with his wire-framed circular spectacles and slight presence, looked anything but the daring rock climber or accomplished athlete:

The secret of his almost unequalled success as a rock-climber was his abnormal finger-power, and an exceptional gift of balance on small foot-holds. – One Christmas time an ice axe was arranged as a horizontal bar, some marvellous feats were shown by experts, but Jones who had been watching retiring from the end of the room came forward and astonished everybody. He grasped the bar with three fingers of his left hand, lifted me with his right arm, and by sheer force of muscular strength raised his chin to the level of the bar three times.

I do not know any rock athletes today able to emulate this feat of strength. To do a three-finger one-arm pull-up while lifting another person of at least equal weight (actually George was of greater stature) is probably impossible. Isn't it?

Then there was local character and landlord Auld Will Ritson. In a farsighted move, Will founded what is now the Wasdale Head Inn in 1856 by obtaining a licence and adapting his Row Foot Farm. At that time it was called the Huntsman's Inn, though it chiefly catered for the new generation of hill users. Will had a razor wit, was full of pranks, and a great raconteur. He knew and loved the fells intimately and was immensely proud of his local roots. He must have imparted much local knowledge and enthusiastic inspiration to the up-and-coming fellsmen who were to base themselves at his hostelry. George Seatree (President of the Fell and Rock Climbing Club 1908–10) made an ascent of an unrecorded route near what is now known as North Climb, mistaking it for Broad Stand. It lies on the Wasdale side of Mickledore, on the edge of the great Scafell Crag. George thought that Will Ritson sought to flatter him when Will, by now getting on in years, insisted:

RIGHT: The Wasdale Head Inn (prominently labelled in case you should miss it), with the snow-flecked shoulder of Looking Stead beyond. The inn was at the centre of early climbing on Scafell and would be packed out every Christmas and Easter holiday. Now boasting a micro-brewery, with a nearby bunkhouse, self-catering accommodation, a climbing shop and a campsite, it remains a focal point for climbers and walkers.

There's nobbut ya way up't Scaafell crags that's be't Broad Strand on't Eshgill [Eskdale] side ot Mickledooer ridge an nowt but a fleein' thing could git up't crags on't Wasdale Head side. Nivver neahbody hed gitten up theer, and neahbody nivyer wad.

Perhaps Auld Will had the truer insight. O. G. Jones, the most gifted and daring climber of his generation, died in the Alps in 1899. In 1903, in an attempt to repeat Jones's 1898 route up the Scafell Pinnacle face, four climbers plunged to their deaths.

But it was not long before one of the most famous climbs in England was pioneered, by Siegfried Herford and George Sansom on 20 April 1914 on the Central Buttress of Scafell. This deserves its place in a general history of the Scafells because its impact transcended a rock climb, however hard. The tale of their final ascent and its aftermath is one of vision and daring, which has inspired generations of mountain people. Its impact on the British psyche is comparable with the loss of Mallory and Irvine on Everest, or of the first ascent of Everest by Tensing and Hillary.

Herford and Sansom met as undergraduates. They formed a superb climbing partnership, though it was undoubtedly Herford who was regarded as the finest climber of his generation. Described as 'incomparable', he made a number of daring climbs in the Peak District and further afield before concentrating his efforts with Sansom on Scafell. He went to Manchester University in 1909, where he excelled in mathematics and technical studies, becoming one of the world's first aeronautical engineers. At the outbreak of World War I he travelled to France to become a war correspondent. After serving as a driver for the Red Cross Society, in 1915 he enlisted in the 24th Royal Fusiliers; he was killed by a rifle grenade on 28 January 1916, aged 24. George Sansom graduated in zoology from University College, London, in 1912. He was of a scientific bent, made much of his own equipment, and was a brilliant photomicrographer. In World War I he served at the front with the St John Ambulance Brigade, before joining the Royal Flying Corps. He was awarded both the MC and the Distinguished Flying Cross, survived the war and lived to the age of 91.

After some initial exploits in 1912, and on further investigation of the Central Buttress with Stanley Jeffcoat (also to die in the war), Herford wrote to Sansom in July 1913. Sansom was rather inconveniently ensconced in the forests of Brazil at the time, but nevertheless this letter decided the future of the greatest rock climbing challenge in Britain. Herford sketched out, in description and drawing, the whole of the route and identified the crux Flake Crack section thus: 'We found that it will go without serious difficulty except the top 20 ft of the flake crack.'

The next year they put theory into practice and indeed found that the crux of the climb was to surmount, from a huge chockstone jammed near the top, the final few grossly overhanging feet of the flake crack. Sansom threaded the rope around the chockstone and attached himself to it while Herford, precariously standing on his shoulders, attempted to reach the top. C. F. Holland, who was also on this first ascent, described the drama:

Sansom was hanging by indifferent sloping handholds on or near the lower end of the great chockstone, and Herford was standing on his shoulders, about to make the first step of the last tremendous solo effort. The initial difficulty confronting him was that of getting a purchase with his left foot in a groove unsuitably shaped for that purpose. Sansom's left hand began to slip under the great strain, and must inevitably have given way very soon, in which case he would have come off, though only for a foot or two, on to the loops. Herford's fall, unavoidable if this had happened, would have been a very serious affair indeed, and even if his rope had held it is impossible to see how we below could have given any assistance, beyond keeping the ropes tight, if either had been injured in any way. . . . Finding himself unable to get his foot as he wanted it, Herford stepped back and accidentally put his foot on the slipping hand, thus holding it in position; and the difficult step was made so quickly at the second attempt that Sansom was able to support the double weight till that of the leader was removed.

Within a few months of this daring ascent, Britain was plunged into war and nothing was to be the same again. One day in 1916, a lone climber descended to Mickledore to take shelter and eat some lunch. From the thin mist rising from below the figure of a young man appeared, with clear-cut face and deep blue eyes; he stopped and they chatted a while. The date was 28 January – the day Siegfried Herford was killed. Stories of sightings of his ghost on Scafell have run ever since. Of course, I could not really subscribe to what is obviously a rather fanciful tale – save for the fact that something rather odd once happened to me. It was 13 November 1982, a cold, sleeting, damp and misty day; the first snows of winter were arriving. I was alone on Scafell Pike, having left my companion to make his own way down from Hollow Stones. Having just ascended to the summit, I had begun to make my way down towards Mickledore. Out of the mists appeared a figure. We greeted each other: he seemed to be a fit young lad of pleasant disposition, and he passed by. He was wearing khaki, which did not strike me as out of the ordinary, since many people on the hill used to wear combat-style clothing. Only, and this did strike me as very odd, he was wearing puttees above his black boots. I am kind of slow with these things and did not give it any thought, until some time later it crossed my mind again. Nobody in the 80s wore puttees – a form of dress confined to early explorers and soldiers of World War I!

After Herford's death, a battle-weary C. F. Holland on leave from the trenches penned this poignant piece:

As the car sped swiftly along the side of the lake it all seemed like a dream. Before me lay Wasdale with its picturesque little hotel in a nest of trees, the quaint cluster of fields looking more than ever like a jig-saw puzzle, and the surrounding hills asleep in the autumn sunshine. . . . In the evening I sat alone and looked at the pictures in the fire, pictures of the 'dear dead days'. How it all came back to me! The happy circle sitting around the fire in this very room, the rapid ebb and flow of conversation, talk of past performances, discussions of plans for the future, anecdote and friendly chaff, followed by absorbing games played with a rope slung over a beam, and attempts at hand balances and other follies fraught with danger to furniture if not to life and limb, until finally someone looks at the time which reminds us that if we would carry out the next day's plans it would be as well for us to get some sleep. . . . And now comes a swiftly moving throng of memories, treading on one another's toes and jostling each other out of the light. . . . All this time there have always been two things above me, a rope, and Herford at the end of it . . . The ultimate bump breaks the spell and all I see now is a face of one who will never again be seen on the rocks he loved so well. . . . His memory will always live as long as rock climbing endures, not only as a great climber, but also as a great-hearted gentleman who gave his life for his country. By many of us he will be remembered as the finest and bravest man we ever knew. . . . May the memory of what he was be a stimulus and an incentive to those who are left to play the game both on the rocks and off them.

Accordingly, events on Central Buttress have always reflected the story of rock climbing itself, both triumph and tragedy. On 28 August 1925, Mabel Barker, partnered by Claude Frankland, one of the great gritstone crack climbers of the time, made only the fourth ascent, and the first by a woman. She had led the top section of the Great Flake, the most difficult of the climb, by squeezing into the crack and climbing inside it rather than on its outside edge. An incredulous team, looking on from the much easier Keswick Brothers climb, were amazed to see Mabel and Claude sitting atop the Great Flake. Mabel noted: 'Probably no lady in history was ever so sure of creating a mild sensation by the mere fact of being where she was.'

In 1931 Menlove Edwards, a powerful climber and one of the most important figures in the history of climbing in Snowdonia, led the route entirely free without sling or rope on the chockstone. Jim Birkett took it one step further by climbing it in nailed boots before climbing down the route in like manner! Alice ('Jammy') Nelson was the first woman to lead the entire route, seconded by her husband-to-be, Sid Cross, on 4 June 1939.

In the 1960s and 70s a character nicknamed 'CB Sid' used to climb solo to the Oval beneath the Great Flake and wait until someone led in front of him. He would then get a rope from above to climb the Flake before unroping and disappearing solo up the rest of the climb. Sid was a lovely character and his ascents of Central Buttress must have run into the hundreds, but he never once led it.

On 18 July 1990, North Yorkshire Moors experts Tony Marr and Mike Tooke made a variation to the climb, moving out on to the open face of the Flake beneath the chockstone. Although spectacularly exposed, the technical difficulty was, amazingly, relatively modest. Little did anyone realise at the time how important and subsequently popular this variation was to become.

Tragically, on 4 June 1994, the huge chockstone fell out of the crack and killed Iain George Newman. He had attempted the Flake and fallen from near the top, though he had been held by his companion Robert Cobbold with the rope passing through a sling on the chockstone. He was lowered back to the Oval, the starting ledge for this pitch, when suddenly the chockstone, which must have weighed a couple of tons, fell from the crack some 15m above.

Throughout the history of these mountains there have been many accidents, as well as incidents of walkers going missing, and all too frequently these events end in tragedy. However, one famous case of 'lost on the fells', the mysterious disappearance of Mr Crump, constitutes perhaps the most remarkable tale of survival ever enacted in British hills. On the morning of 21 June 1921, one Mr E. C. Crump, a man in his fifties, set forth from Fell Foot in Little Langdale. His overall scheme was to walk from Tilberthwaite to Crummock Water. Unfortunately, he failed to detail the route which he intended to follow, and there are many possibilities and variations. When Mr Crump failed to reappear, extensive searches were activated; on one day alone, some thirty members of the Fell and Rock Climbing Club scoured the wilds of Bowfell. All in vain – Mr Crump joined the 'missing persons' category. Few if anyone expected to find him alive again.

The weather that summer, however, was remarkably warm and dry. A. R. Thompson of Keswick, a member of the Alpine Club and a noted cragsman, decided that the notorious Piers Gill should be sufficiently dry to attempt an ascent. To date it had received only two ascents and was one of the least popular routes in the region. Tucked away near the very head of Wasdale, the huge rift of this gill, with vertical pitches which are generally free-falling waterfalls, nestles beneath the cliffs of Lingmell. It does, however, lie directly beneath the well-trodden path along the Corridor Route which leads from the Lingmoor col, traversing the flanks of the Scafells to reach Styhead Pass. In short, in poor visibility it is all too easy to enter the head of the rift by mistake.

Leading a team of two other climbers, Thompson made good progress up the gill, and after climbing a steep waterfall pitch was surprised when he saw a person below, sitting precariously balanced on the edge of a small ledge. Initially Thompson thought it must be a member of his own group who had perhaps decided to descend rather than advance up the difficult climb. However, when the rest of his team arrived, it became all too obvious that it was someone else below. Somehow, in the deep confines of the gully, engaged in the difficulty of climbing, they had gone past the figure without seeing him. Thompson and his two companions descended, to find it was a man and he was alive. Unbelievably, it was the hapless Mr Crump. The date was 9 July and he had been stuck alone in the gully for eighteen days – almost three weeks of isolation, discomfort and starvation!

On the fateful day that Crump left Little Langdale, he had ascended Wrynose Pass and traversed the Crinkles, Bowfell and Esk Pike before falling to Esk Hause. Apparently, at this point, he had intended to descend to Styhead, but the day being fair he changed his mind and decided to scale Scafell Pike instead. As night fell, mist and clouds began to roll in and Crump became disorientated. He stumbled towards the head of Piers Gill with no idea where he was. Instead of bearing off right on the Corridor Route he took a line left of the head of the gill and attempted descent. On the scree-strewn, steep ground among the cliffs of Lingmell, he slipped and plunged into the depths of the gill, badly injuring both ankles. With vertical rock above and below him and confined by the steep walls of the gully, he was trapped with no way out. His only food was one sandwich and a small piece of gingerbread. He divided these into six pieces and had 'a mouthful for six days'; after that, he had only a trickle of water to keep him alive. With all this, he had the fortitude to make rough notes in case at some point his remains might be discovered.

Crump was found at 4.30 p.m. and Thompson and his party had him down to the Wasdale Head Inn by 10.30 p.m. This remarkable tale of survival says mountains for Mr Crump's mental and physical determination, if not for his powers of navigation. That first pint must have been truly wonderful!

Perhaps there is something special about Piers Gill: in March 1978 another incident occurred which most would have expected to end in tragedy. A Piper Cherokee flying from Southport to Carlisle got caught in a storm and went missing. Coincidentally, a party from Watford Grammar School were making their way through heavy mist when they

came across a man who said that he had just crawled out of a crashed aeroplane. Unlikely as this may have seemed, sure enough, a little way distant lay the wreckage of the plane and his two companions. Though injured, all three from the Piper Cherokee survived, their impact having being cushioned by a deep bank of snow.

Few rescues can have been more spectacular than the one that unfolded on the Esk Buttress during the spring of 1991. Two climbers – Glen Wilks, who was leading, and Pete Strong – were on an extreme route called Microbe, put up by Rick Graham and myself back in 1982. Suddenly, Glen fell and was catapulted into space – he thought later that a tiny foothold had broken. Though held on the ropes by Pete it was a painful fall, and Glen felt as though his ribs were broken. Pete secured Glen on a ledge, then made descent down the cliff before running all the way down into Eskdale to the public telephone near Brotherilkeld. A little later a Sea King helicopter arrived on the scene and began to hover inches away from the crag so that rescue team members could be lowered to Glen, the usual practice whereby the injured person would be secured to a cable and winched to safety by the helicopter. But as team member outward bound instructor Judith Cantrel was being lowered, the tip of the rotor blade of the hovering helicopter touched the cliff. Everyone's worst nightmare began to unfold. Glen reported:

> It was horrific. Rocks, shale, debris, bits of metal rained down on top of us on the tiny ledge. And the noise. I just knew this great mass of Sea King was likely to drop like a stone and squash us flat.

The helicopter managed to bank away, but it could only be a matter of seconds before it would be forced to crash-land on Great Moss below. Meanwhile, like a rag doll whizzed around on the end of a piece of string, Judith

ABOVE: At the very head of Wasdale, beyond the hamlet of Wasdale Head, the deep rift of Piers Gill rises towards the east face of Lingmell.

Cantrel was still hanging from the cable beneath the stricken helicopter. The winchman had the option to fire an explosive shear-cutter to sever the cable and let Judith fall to the ground. But the extraordinary skill of the pilot, and the nerve and judgement of the winchman, enabled the helicopter to stay airborne just long enough to get her inside. A split second later, it crashed into Great Moss – yet, unbelievably, everyone inside survived. Later, high on the crag, a group of climbers managed to lower Glen to the bottom and get him away from the cliff; a second helicopter carried him safely to Whitehaven Hospital. How fortunate was that?

***

I have always felt it is both a right and a privilege to enjoy activities on the mountains. However, with this philosophy must come a great deal of personal responsibility – to ourselves, to others and to the precious and delicate environment. It is fatuous for anyone to claim that they own mountains or wild places. For them to be managed in trust by responsible bodies, who promote the best interests of the general public and care for the mountain environment and its natural habitat, is a somewhat different matter. The Scafells are now 'owned' and managed by the National Trust and come under the general responsibility of the Lake District National Park Authority.

Historically, this came about in four stages. In 1920, the 3rd Lord Leconfield gave 40 acres to the National Trust as a war memorial for the Lake District. In 1923, the Fell and Rock Climbing Club gifted 1,184 acres to the National Trust, including the heights both north and south of Styhead Pass, with Great Gable, Great End, Broad Crag and Lingmell. In 1924, some 1,310 acres above 609m (the 2,000ft mark) were bought from Lord Leconfield by Gordon Wordsworth, the poet's grandson, and A. C. Benson, a Cambridge don, prolific essayist and critic, who loved and often walked in the area. Both were early members of the Trust, and passed the land on to the Trust in 1925. A plaque on the summit records their 'dedication' to the nation. Leconfield himself was baffled:

> I can't see why you should want to buy – you can go anywhere, do anything already. I have no rights but mineral and shooting rights; and there isn't an ounce of anything but soft stone, nor any sign of life . . . Still, if you have money to throw away and like to buy rights which you already enjoy, well and good.

Finally, to complete the Trust's ownership of the Scafells, the Leconfield Commons were transferred in 1979 through National Land Fund Procedures. The Trust is now custodian of the whole of this magnificent landscape.

Through good management and our support it is to be hoped that this will guarantee free open access, while conserving natural beauty for all time.

In the 1980s the National Trust began rebuilding footpaths which had become badly eroded. The first supervisor of the footpath building team was a climbing friend of mine called Ray McHaffie. Mac was one of the great characters of the Lakeland climbing scene. From the gangs of Raffles, the notorious slums of Carlisle (now demolished), he turned his life around to live in Keswick and climb prolifically in Borrowdale. His enthusiasm for climbing and the hills knew no bounds. One summer we lectured together at the Moot Hall in Keswick (Mac continued this for years), showing slides of climbing and the landscape of the area. Within a few moments Mac would have the audience in stitches. The hall was always packed and eventually we had to do two showings to cater for the numbers. Some of his sayings were unforgettable. On talking about some climbing disaster: 'Aye it was terrible, in fact they were both seriously killed.' On modern hard climbers: 'You can always tell an Extreme Climber: if you look carefully, they all have little wings under their tee-shirts.'

Mac and his gang built the footpath up Grains Gill and in 1987 he rebuilt the crumbling summit cairn. He also constructed the stone zigzags, now rapidly disintegrating, above Fox's Tarn. During the summit works, he and his gang slept on the mountain. One morning when they arrived for work they found the unfortunate victim of a suicide attempt in a bad way among the stones of the summit cairn. Mac kept him alive until the Wasdale Mountain Rescue team arrived.

In this short record of man's involvement with the Scafells, I have aimed to show that this is a special place which has involved and captivated many, something more than just an inanimate pile of stone that happens to be the highest ground in England. George Sansom, pioneer of the great Central Buttress, died at the ripe old age of 91. Next to him when he died, marked in pencil, were the lines of a poem by Geoffrey Winthrop Young. For those of us fortunate enough to have been involved with this magnificent mountain, I think it sums up our feelings nicely:

> What if I live no more those kingly days?
>   their night sleeps with me still.
> I dream my feet upon the starry ways;
>   my heart rests in the hill.
> I may not grudge the little left undone:
> I hold the heights, I keep the dreams I won.

> Geoffrey Winthrop Young, 'On High Hills'

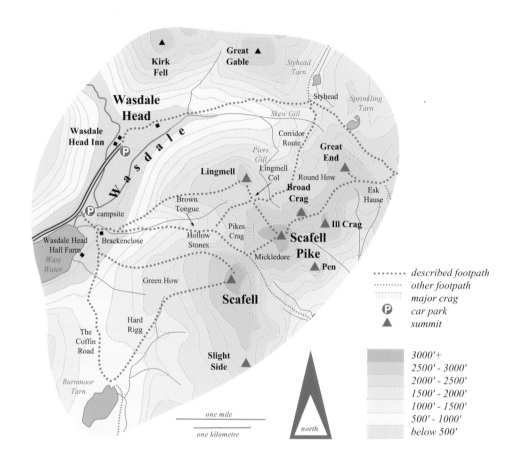

described footpath
other footpath
major crag
Ⓟ **car park**
▲ **summit**

one mile
one kilometre

north

3000'+
2500' - 3000'
2000' - 2500'
1500' - 2000'
1000' - 1500'
500' - 1000'
below 500'

Great End *Lingmell* *Broad Crag* *Scafell Pike* *Mickledore* *Scafell* *Slight Side*

*RIGHT AND OPPOSITE:
Yewbarrow provides one of the
best vistas of the northern side
of the Scafell Massif. Beyond
the bulk of Lingmell in the
foreground, the full length of
the range can be seen from
here. Great End lies at the
north-eastern extent to the left,
while Slight Side, at the south-
western limit, is the little
protuberance to the right.*

Surrounded by high impressive fells,
Wasdale's heady atmosphere is unparalleled.
It provides the most direct access to Lingmell,
Scafell Pike and Scafell, and for climbers the
quickest ascent to Pikes Crag, the great cliffs
of Scafell Crags and the East Buttress.

THE APPROACHES FROM
WASDALE

Despite its relatively remote location near the western fringes of Cumbria, Wasdale has long been the mountain sanctuary from which climbers and walkers approach the Scafells. Surrounded by high impressive fells and positioned at the foot of Britain's highest mountain Massif, its heady atmosphere is unparalleled. For those seeking the tops, it provides the most direct access to Lingmell, Scafell Pike and Scafell. For climbers, usually via the slog up Brown Tongue and through Hollow Stones, it provides the quickest ascent to Pikes Crag and the great cliffs of Scafell Crags, and the East Buttress on the Eskdale side of Mickledore.

Many routes begin just above the head of Wast Water lake, at the small car park beside the campsite, a little lower down the valley than Wasdale Head itself. The banks of Lingmell Gill are followed, past the wonderfully located Fell and Rock Climbing Club Hut of Brackenclose. The path along the true left bank of the beck passes through the oaks fringing Brackenclose and by the whin bushes, complete with golden blossom in early spring, until a footbridge leads to the true right bank. Above this a gate and kissing gate lead to a splitting of the ways.

The path ascending the nose of Lingmell breaks off left. This provides ascent up a long open ridge; beyond the high stile, which crosses the fell wall, it offers excellent views over Wast Water and the valley of Wasdale. Levelling beyond the steepest section of the nose, the path continues to the little craggy outcrops of Goat Crags. It leads more or less directly though these, before bearing left to climb to the summit rocks and the circular cairn of Lingmell. The summit occupies a strategic position in a fine mountain location – for those with limited time, it should be considered as a worthy top in its own right. Despite its open aspect and fine views, it is a surprisingly quiet route.

The most popular ascent, because it is the most direct, is to continue along the well-blazoned rough track above Lingmell Gill. Rocky in places, it rises through the mixed woods flanking the beck to emerge, through a kissing gate, on to the open fellside. A little higher and the path crosses the clear sparkling beck via the boulders separating the cascades. The nose of Brown Tongue lies directly above. It is a notorious slog, and the chief recommendation for it is its directness. Recent erosion control measures have made the ascent easier; there is now a footpath up the right side so that the nose of the ridge can be avoided. At the bottom, just above the beck, is a ruined rectangular structure with a wonderful outlook over Wast Water far below. A similar structure, located at roughly the same altitude, is to be found out towards the nose of Lingmell.

At the top of Brown Tongue lies the lovely basin of Hollow Stones, often used by climbers as an unofficial high mountain camp. Many have spent sublime evenings here, the huge sweep of Scafell Crags bathed in evening sunshine above while Wasdale stretches out far below. The way splits here, with a new track going off left for the ascent to Lingmell Col. Constructed with the help of a mini-excavator flown in by helicopter, its smooth snake-like length, twisting up the fellside, looks uncomfortably out of place in this wild mountain environment.

The climber's route continues with another steep ascent to the corrie directly below Scafell Crags, marked by the shelter boulder perched on the lip of its lower rim. A useful little stream below provides a drink and the chance to replenish water bottles. Directly across this stony cove and up the steep scree forming its head lies the col of Mickledore, the low ridge that joins Scafell Pike to Scafell.

Overlooking the cove on the left is the attractive Pikes Crag (labelled Pulpit Rock on the Ordnance Survey map although seldom referred to as such), while above the steep scree to the right is the huge face of Scafell Crags. Direct ascent of this scree, with the crag of Shamrock falling to the right, leads directly to the base of Scafell Pinnacle. Athough unstable, and not particularly pleasant, this is one of the regular approaches for walkers wishing to access Lord's Rake or the West Wall Traverse.

Those wishing to continue to Scafell Pike from the shelter stone may either traverse left, crossing the hillside by a narrow path beneath Pikes Crag and so out to Lingmell Col, or continue straight ahead, following the path through the basin before making the steep ascent directly up the scree to Mickledore. This is the route most favoured by climbers wishing to gain Mickledore as quickly as possible, but it is steep and eroded at the top and not particularly enjoyable for walkers.

Other routes also start by Brackenclose at the foot of the mountain. The Green How path, which starts by traversing beneath the climbing hut, offers a much less strenuous approach to Scafell, both in terms of a shallower ascent and an easier, grassier terrain below the feet. Before it passes above Wasdale Head Hall Farm, a path branches off left to climb directly up the flank of the hillside. Beyond the fell wall, as the angle begins to ease, it veers off left to follow the shoulder of Green How; it is intercepted by the top of the Lord's Rake route, which comes in from the left before continuing to the summit ridge of Scafell. Once a favourite route to the summit, it is now relatively little used for the ascent but remains popular for the descent. To locate it from above, follow the north-west arm of the stone cross in the hollow below the rocky knoll of Deep Ghyll Buttress (marked as Symonds Knott on the Ordnance Survey map).

A further route takes the Wasdale to Eskdale 'coffin road' towards high Burnmoor Tarn to the point where it is possible to head off left, ascending the shoulder of Hard Rigg above Hardrigg Gill. Views from this route extend over Burnmoor Tarn and down secretive Miterdale as well as over the head of Wast Water. Probably one of the kindest ascents, it is thought to be the route taken by Coleridge in 1802.

The way from Wasdale Head up the packhorse route to Styhead has long been a popular and worthy approach to the Scafells – for many, it is *the* route to Scafell Pike. It climbs from the valley floor to traverse the vast scree-strewn flanks of Great Gable while soaking in the mountain atmosphere around the very head of Wasdale: to the right the dark side of Lingmell and the black depths of Piers Gill; ahead the formidable rents and crags that make up the inhospitable north-west face of Great End. Once the col of Styhead is reached the way is open either to traverse around to Esk Hause or to follow the Corridor Route leading to Lingmell Col. For those

ABOVE: The fell wall crossed by the style leading to the steepest section of the nose that rises from Wasdale to the top of Lingmell. I once carried my daughter in a backpack up here: she enjoyed it! The highest top seen beyond is Pillar above the darkness of Mosedale.

wishing to climb only Scafell Pike, the Corridor Route provides the shortest option.

The Corridor Route traverses the huge ruggedness of the north-west steeps of Great End. At first appearance it can be hard to identify, but in execution it all falls into place. A cairn at the southern end of the connecting ridge of Styhead marks the start; bearing right at this point to make a slight descent begins what is, in effect, a long diagonal traverse of the mountainside. The way is well worn, though there are a few key sections where it is imperative not to lose the path. The first deep rift to cross is Skew Gill (which skewers the flanks of Great End); immediately afterwards, a steep ascent is made by the south edge of the ravine before the way moves off right again.

The path climbs rightwards to pass above the top of the buttress known as Stand Crag before it crosses the narrow head of a deep gully – in effect, this is the far left branch of Piers Gill. It continues to traverse beneath the craggy slopes of Round How, crossing Greta Gill above the deep ravine and finally crossing the true head of the notorious Piers Gill. A large drop and a spectacular waterfall lie just below – great care is required. From here the path begins to make a steeper ascent. From just beyond the head of the gill, one path rises directly to the col between Broad Crag and Scafell Pike – steep, rough and not recommended. The main route bears right from here until the way again steepens and bears left to climb directly towards the summit dome of Scafell Pike. Those wishing to gain Lingmell Col should bear off right before the steep ascent, to join and follow the line of a ruined stone wall. The beehive-shaped summit cairn of Lingmell lies to the right (north), some 76m above the col. Scafell Pike lies to the left (south), some 244m higher.

BELOW: Nearing the head of Wast Water, the view over the lake opens to the heart of the Scafells and the hanging corrie of Hollow Stones. The cliffs of Shamrock and Scafell Crag stand to the right and Pikes Crag to the left. This view, at the very head of the lake, opens out above the charming mountain hut of Brackenclose, the Wasdale base of the Fell and Rock Climbing Club.

BELOW: The drive up the
mountain valley of Wasdale is
one of the finest in the whole
Lake District, offering ever-
changing and wonderful views
of the Western Fells. In this
scene, looking over Wast Water
to Wasdale Head Hall Farm,
Scafell is dominant. Lingmell,,
topped by Scafell Pike, stands
to the left and the great
shoulder of Scafell to the right.

OPPOSITE: A perfect end to another perfect day on Scafell, with a wonderful furnace-red light cast by a rapidly setting sun. By the time I reached Brackenclose it was dark. This view looks back up the path at a point just below the crossing of Lingmell Gill and the steep ribbon of Brown Tongue.

BELOW: Middle Fell provides this open aspect of the Massif above the head of Wast Water. The notch on the skyline is Mickledore, with Scafell Pike to the left and Scafell to the right. This is probably the feature noted by William Wilberforce when he wrote in 1779 of 'a high hill with a kind of crack in it – said by the people thereabouts to be higher than Skiddaw.'

ABOVE: Helped by a dusting of snow, a long lens from the valley floor heightens the dramatic effect of the cliffs which guard the summits of the Scafells. The sweep of Shamrock stands to the right and Pikes Crag, seamed by gullies, to the left.

LEFT: The little basin of Hollow Stones provides a pleasant refuge for climbers staying the night on Scafell. It also marks the parting of the ways, with one path leading off to Lingmell col, the other continuing to make strenuous ascent direct to Mickledore.

OPPOSITE: Rising out of Lingmell Gill, the rib of Brown Tongue leads to Hollow Stones. Although a notorious slog, Brown Tongue nevertheless provides the shortest route to the heights from Wasdale, with an excellent pitched path now climbing along its right side.

ABOVE: A curtain of ice hangs from Shamrock, while cloud hangs above Mosedale.

LEFT: This large boulder, well known to climbers as a place to shelter and bivouac, lies just above Hollow Stones at the lip of the upper hanging corrie beneath the crags of Scafell and Scafell Pike. A natural spring can be found just below whose sweet waters never seem to dry even in the driest of summers. The point of Pikes Crag forms the backdrop.

ABOVE: Evening light casts colour on the boulder-strewn summit dome of Scafell Pike. The most popular path to and from this point leads to Lingmell Col.

RIGHT: Looking from the rocky top of Deep Ghyll Buttress (marked as Symonds Knott on the Ordnance Survey map) down to the head of Wast Water, the starting point for many of the walks up Scafell Pike and Scafell.

*BELOW: Wasdale Head,
complete with church, inn,
bunkhouse, campsite, mountain
shop and car park, retains a
distinctive patchwork field
system defined by stone
boundary walls. Looking down
on the hamlet from the flanks
of Yewbarrow, Kirkfell stands
to the left, Lingmell to the right
and Great Gable in the centre.
The path leading over the
flanks of Gable to Styhead
provides one of the pleasantest
approaches to the Scafell
heights.*

BELOW: The path in the
foreground is the main route
rising across the flanks of Great
Gable to climb from Wasdale
Head to Styhead – not the
shortest but arguably one of
the nicest approaches from
Wasdale to the Scafells. The
great hulking fellside beyond
is Great End and close
examination, where light enters
the shadow, reveals the Corridor
Route traversing and climbing
from the col of Styhead to the
col of Lingmell (out of picture).

BELOW: Blue remembered hills: Scafell profiled above Lingmell, seen from Kirkfell on an autumn afternoon.

OPPOSITE: Looking over Wasdale Head and the flanks of Lingmell to the sun's silvery reflection in Wast Water. It is easy to see why the tiny hamlet of Wasdale Head, surrounded by mountains, has long been a mecca for mountaineers, climbers and hill walkers.

BELOW: The rocky dome of Round How, dwarfed by Great End behind, tends to blend with the fellside until lit by the evening sun.

OPPOSITE: The high ground of Styhead separates the valleys of Wasdale and Borrowdale. This view, from the Corridor Route, looks over to tranquil Styhead Tarn and down into a darkening Borrowdale.

LEFT: Lingmell's summit cairn and rocks with a bit of Great Gable seen to the right. The top of Lingmell is a very fine viewpoint and was once very fashionable; today, it is mainly passed by those with eyes only for the highest point in England – Scafell Pike.

BELOW: A ruined stone wall and scattering of blocks on Lingmell Col. Looking up the rocky slopes of Scafell Pike, Dropping Crag can be seen at the top left.

BELOW: Shafts of evening sunshine rake across Lingmell Col at the head of the Corridor Route. Middleboot Knotts can be seen centrally with the slopes of Scafell Pike rising behind.

BELOW: From Lingmell Col to
the slopes of Scafell (plunging
to Wasdale) at sunset.

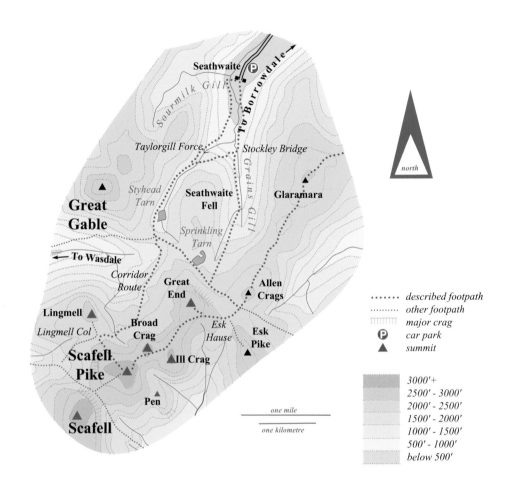

described footpath
.... other footpath
|||||||| major crag
Ⓟ car park
▲ summit

3000'+
2500' - 3000'
2000' - 2500'
1500' - 2000'
1000' - 1500'
500' - 1000'
below 500'

one mile
one kilometre

Sourmilk Gill

Seathwaite Ⓟ

To Borrowdale ➤

Taylorgill Force   *Stockley Bridge*

Grains Gill

▲

**Great
Gable**

*Styhead
Tarn*

**Seathwaite
Fell**

Glaramara ▲

*Sprinkling
Tarn*

← **To Wasdale**

*Corridor
Route*

**Great
End**

**Allen
Crags** ▲

Lingmell ▲

Lingmell Col

**Broad
Crag**

▲

*Esk
Hause*

**Esk
Pike**

**Scafell
Pike**

▲ **Ill Crag**

Pen ▲

▲ **Scafell**

north

Ill Crag   Great End   Lingmell

RIGHT AND OPPOSITE: Great
End from Glaramara, with the
black scar of Central Gully
prominent. Ill Crag stands to the
left and Lingmell to the right.

The more adventurous route to reach
Styhead Tarn takes in the spectacular
waterfall of Taylorgill Force – this is
undoubtedly the more scenic approach.

THE APPROACHES FROM
BORROWDALE

All the best routes from Borrowdale to the Scafells start from the head of Seathwaite, passing through Seathwaite Farm. This starting point also serves numerous other popular mountains, notably Great Gable. As there is no car park hereabouts, on any weekend in summer or winter a long string of cars lines the roadside leading to the farm.

There are two fundamental lines of approach – either via Grains Gill to bear left beneath Great End to gain Esk Hause, or to ascend to Styhead before either passing Sprinkling Tarn and Great End to gain Esk Hause or to proceed along the Corridor Route to Lingmell Col (see the approaches from Wasdale). From the farm, the main track leads directly up the valley to the stone-arched packhorse Stockley Bridge before splitting left up Grains Gill or right to Styhead Tarn and hence to Styhead.

However, there is a more adventurous route to Styhead Tarn, undoubtedly the most scenic, taking in the spectacular waterfall of Taylorgill Force. A roofed opening in the farmyard leads through the barn on the right via a footbridge over Seathwaite Beck to the foot of Sourmilk Gill. From here the path follows the right (true left) bank of the beck, to make a rocky scramble (for adventurous walkers only) past Taylorgill Force and then along by the banks of Styhead Gill.

The masochistic, or supremely fit, who seek a challenge may wish to start up the lane which leads off the main valley road by Mountain View Cottages/Strands Bridge towards Thorneythwaite Farm (there is a parking area). This is a high-level route of continual and great interest. The way lies up Thorneythwaite Fell to gain the tops of Glaramara before proceeding south along the high ridge leading over Allen Crags before dropping to Esk Hause.

BELOW: Crossing the stone cobbles of Seathwaite Farm, Borrowdale's gateway to the Scafells.

ABOVE: Looking to Taylorgill Force from Seathwaite valley. The waterfall is spectacular and, though it involves a short section of moderate scrambling, provides an excellent route to Styhead. To get on the right path, it is necessary to pass through the flat archway in the buildings of Seathwaite Farm.

RIGHT: Stockley Bridge, beyond which the Borrowdale paths to Scafell split up to Grains Gill or Styhead Tarn. This is a typical Lakeland packhorse bridge on what was once a main route from the inner Lake District to the west coast, taking out Seathwaite wad, a pure natural graphite, and bringing in brandy and rum. Seems like a good exchange!

*ABOVE: Ascending by Grains
Gill towards the snow-clad
north face of Great End is the
most direct route to the Massif
from Borrowdale. Special care
should be taken in icy
conditions, however.*

BELOW: Styhead Tarn is traversed by a path which serves as the main route to both the Scafell Massif and Great Gable. In a relatively sheltered hollow, it provides an ideal 'unofficial' high mountain campsite. Beyond can be seen Great End to the left, Broad Crag and Scafell Pike in the centre and Lingmell to the right.

OPPOSITE: Reflections of Great End, Lingmell and Great Gable in the tranquil waters of Styhead Tarn. In late spring, the mayfly larvae start to hatch here, which can result in a brown trout feeding frenzy, usually at its most intense during early morning and late evening, when the tarn's surface can be a myriad of expanding rings.

RIGHT: A classic view, looking down on the pocket handkerchief of Styhead Tarn from the shoulder of Great Gable. Spout Head and the deep rent of Skew Gill, traversed by the Corridor Route, are seen to the right.

BELOW: Leaving the summit plateau of Great Gable, with a view to Sprinkling Tarn nestling beneath Great End. Esk Hause and Allen Crags can be seen in the middle distance, beyond which lies the head of the Great Langdale valley.

BELOW: I took this shot looking to Styhead Tarn and Great Gable while making an ascent up the north face of Great End. Let me take this opportunity to thank all the many climbing companions I have asked to tarry while I have framed an irresistible image – I salute their patience!

BELOW: Looking to Allen Crags over Esk Hause, with the famed cross-walled shelter by the intersection of the paths. Esk Hause is the highest mountain pass in England, the point at which the routes from Borrowdale, Wasdale, Langstrath, Great Langdale and Eskdale all join before climbing the final leg to the Scafell Massif.

OVERLEAF: From the rocky Scafell Pike summit dome looking north-east to Styhead Tarn. Borrowdale and Derwent Water are seen stretching to Skiddaw and Blencathra beyond.

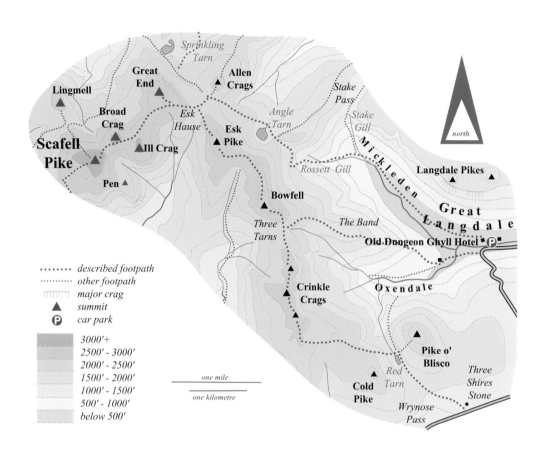

Sprinkling Tarn

Great End

Allen Crags

Lingmell

Broad Crag

Esk Hause

Stake Pass

Stake Gill

Scafell Pike

Ill Crag

Esk Pike

Angle Tarn

north

Pen

Rossett Gill

Langdale Pikes

Mickleden

Great Langdale

Bowfell

Three Tarns

The Band

Old Dungeon Ghyll Hotel ●Ⓟ■

■

.... described footpath

.... other footpath

▦ major crag

▲ summit

Ⓟ car park

Oxendale

Crinkle Crags

3000'+

2500' - 3000'

2000' - 2500'

1500' - 2000'

1000' - 1500'

500' - 1000'

below 500'

one mile

one kilometre

Pike o' Blisco

Three Shires Stone

Red Tarn

Cold Pike

Wrynose Pass

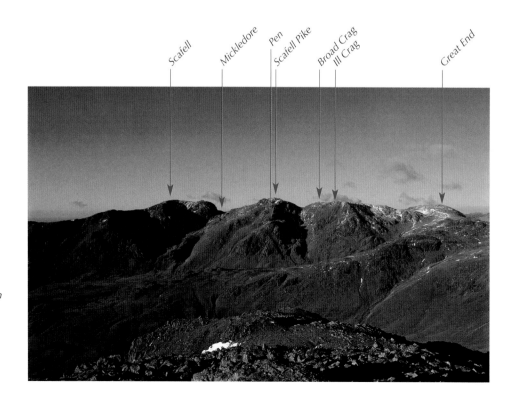

Scafell   Mickledore   Pen   Scafell Pike   Broad Crag   Ill Crag   Great End

RIGHT AND OPPOSITE:
The Scafell Massif viewed from
Long Top, the highest top on
Langdale's Crinkle Crags. The
ridge in the middle ground is
Pike de Bield which climbs
from the bottom of Lingcove
to Esk Pike.

The classic long-distance approach through a sublime mountain landscape, with stunning views to Bowfell and Langdale Pikes, Angle Tarn and Esk Pike, even before you arrive at Esk Hause and the Scafell Massif.

THE APPROACHES FROM
LANGDALE

This is the classic long-distance approach through a sublime mountain landscape, with stunning views to Bowfell and Langdale Pikes, Angle Tarn and Esk Pike, even before you arrive at Esk Hause and the Scafell Massif. Dreams are made of this. Climbers who wish to savour the mountain experience and take on the challenge of the steeps of Scafell should follow this route in the knowledge that, as well as time spent actually climbing, something like seven hours should be added to the day for approach and return.

The most common valley route is from the Old Dungeon Ghyll Hotel (the car park is generally full before 9 a.m. on a summer weekend). The stony track leads beyond its enclosing stone walls to gain the open greensward of Mickleden. It is easy walking along this long, flat, lonely valley, with Mickleden Beck to the left and the sweeping rocks of Gimmer Crag, the Great Stone Shoot and Pike o'Stickle standing to the right, leading to the wooden footbridge over Stake Gill. Piles of stones, evidence of much prehistoric activity, litter the ground on both sides of the path.

Just over the bridge stands a stone sheepfold, at which point Stake Pass, crossing to Langstrath in Borrowdale, rises steeply to the right. The way to Scafell lies straight on with a gentle ascent at first, leading to the deep rift of Rossett Gill renting the head of Mickleden. As the way steepens, it is best to keep out of the bouldery and insecure confines of the ravine to follow the zigzags of the old packhorse route winding its way up the hillside to the left. Near the elbow of one of the zags lies the ancient cross of the Packhorse-

woman's Grave – allegedly she once supplied goods to the farms of Langdale and was buried here in the 1790s, but the real story of this poignant memorial is lost in the mists of time.

Descent from the head of the gill and the shoulder of Rossett Pike leads to the dark and powerful waters of Angle Tarn, another favourite high-mountain camp for those with a sense of romantic adventure and no fear of ghosts. Reasonable ascent from here leads to Esk Hause.

A number of high-level routes may be followed from the Langdales to the Scafells. The most logical of these lies along the high south-western skyline running around the head of Great Langdale. It can be reached in many different ways, though the most logical route, involving a minimum of ascent, begins at the Three Shires Stone standing at the head of Little Langdale. A pretty good track leads first to Red Tarn before the meat arrives. This takes the form of traversing the rugged heights of Crinkle Crags, Bowfell and Esk Pike before finally falling to Esk Hause – a demanding mountain approach, with some of the finest views to the Scafells, a trip that compares with any mountain expedition in Britain. It should be started at sunrise and the return made by moonlight. Anyone experiencing this route must surely be placed in the category defined by Coleridge's conclusion to 'Kubla Khan':

> For he on honey-dew hath fed,
> And drunk the milk of paradise.

BELOW: The Old Dungeon Ghyll Hotel lies at the driveable head of Great Langdale. It is a traditional inn for walkers and climbers, with a long history and tremendous ambience. The attached National Trust public car park fills up rapidly in summer: that and the fact that it is a long walk to the Scafells means an early start is advisable.

OPPOSITE: Looking up Mickleden, the head of Great Langdale, with Langdale Pikes to the right. Allen Crags forms the head of the valley and just beyond (out of picture) is Great End. The white buildings at the bottom right are the Old Dungeon Ghyll Hotel, the best starting point for those heading to the Scafells.

OVERLEAF: The central rib descending to Great Langdale is the Band, the most popular and direct approach for those ascending Bowfell. Oxendale lies to its left, with the white-topped Crinkle Crags above, and Mickleden to its right.

OPPOSITE: The track leading up Mickleden towards Rossett Gill, the most direct and popular approach to the Scafells from Great Langdale.

RIGHT: A migrant Ring Ouzel has caught a worm. With a prominent white collar and distinctive, clear, piping song, it is also known as the mountain blackbird. It is one of the most distinctive birds of the high Scafells between April and September.

BELOW: A wooden footbridge and circular sheepfold mark the point at which the path bifurcates. Right leads over Stake Pass into the head of Borrowdale's Langstrath; left continues to Rossett Gill and on to Esk Hause and the Scafells.

ABOVE: Rossett Gill, at the head of Mickleden, cleaves a deep rent into the fellside. It is best to keep out of the gill itself since it is steep, unstable and badly eroded at the top. The main path, a series of extended zigzags, climbs to the left of the gill and is much the pleasantest way to take. The nicely shaped top to the right is Rossett Pike.

LEFT: In a quiet spot above the zigzags beside Rossett Gill lies the curious array of stones known as the Packhorsewoman's Grave. Please do not disturb her: she has most probably rested here since the eighteenth century. Once all the valleys were served by packhorses carrying in goods from the busy ports of the West Coast and taking out wool and other local produce – including Lanty Slee's whiskey, illicitly distilled in Little Langdale.

OPPOSITE: The view down Mickleden from the head of the zigzags beside Rossett Gill, a welcome sight for those returning home from a traverse of the Scafells. Langdale Pikes stand to the left and dead ahead is the worthy Lingmoor Fell. In the days of limited road travel, Langdale was a popular starting point for climbers heading for Scafell Crag, despite the distance – carrying ropes and equipment there made for a very long day.

BELOW: On the main path dropping from the head of Rossett Gill, directly beneath Ore Gap, little Angle Tarn nestles in the folds between Bowfell and Esk Pike. One hard freezing night I could not understand why the tarn had not frozen – it appeared as just a dead flat surface of black water. Only after throwing a stone and seeing it skidding across the surface did I realise that the water was in fact frozen solid. So still was the night, without a breath of wind, that the ice had formed like a pane of glass, perfectly flat and transparent.

BELOW: The main path,
following the joining of ways,
runs across the flanks of Great
End rising from Esk Hause
into Calf Cove, before finally
ascending to the backbone of
the Massif. This photograph
was taken while descending
the shoulder of Esk Pike.

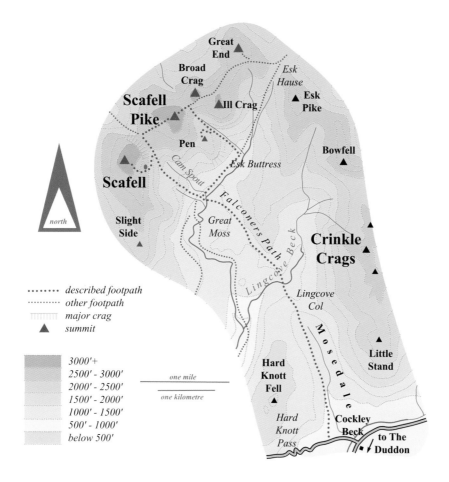

Great
End

Broad
Crag

*Esk
Hause*

**Scafell
Pike**

▲Ill Crag

▲ Esk
Pike

Pen

Esk Buttress

Bowfell
▲

Scafell

Cam Spout

Falconers Path

Slight
Side

*Great
Moss*

Lingcove Beck

**Crinkle
Crags**

*Lingcove
Col*

········· *described footpath*
·········· *other footpath*
⊤⊤⊤⊤⊤⊤ *major crag*
▲ *summit*

north

	3000'+
	2500' - 3000'
	2000' - 2500'
	1500' - 2000'
	1000' - 1500'
	500' - 1000'
	below 500'

one mile

one kilometre

Mosedale

Hard
Knott
Fell
▲

Little
Stand
▲

*Hard
Knott
Pass*

**Cockley
Beck**

**to The
Duddon**

Slight Side

Scafell

Scafell Pike
Pen
Broad Crag
Ill Crag

Great End

*RIGHT AND OPPOSITE:
Looking north-north-west over
the Duddon's Cockley Beck
and up Mosedale to the Scafell
Massif from Grey Friar.*

This feels like the wildest, most remote way of all to explore the Scafells. The pleasure in walking this route, and the longing for it, seems somehow stronger than all the rest.

THE APPROACHES FROM
DUDDON

This feels like the wildest, most remote way of all to explore the Scafells. It is a favoured route for climbers heading for the Esk Buttress, but few walkers know its secrets. It begins just above Cockley Beck, at the foot of Hardknott Pass, following the track into desolate Mosedale.

At the head of little Mosedale, where the path disappears into bog, it is usual to get your feet wet, high or low, whichever route is chosen to gain the Lingcove Col. The view to the heights of the Scafells and the top of the rock monolith of Esk Buttress from this point, though partially obscured by the foreground, is truly inspirational. If this does not set your pulse running, nothing will.

Descent leads to a boulder-hopping crossing of Lingcove Beck. From here a narrow path climbs to a traverse beneath Long Crag. Indefinite and undulating, this nevertheless leads magically to the Great Moss, a desolate and deserted landscape which occupies the very head of Eskdale, and above which is arrayed the whole of the Scafell Massif (save for distant Great End).

I first came this way with my father, following what we called the 'Falconer's Path' to Cam Spout. I still thrill at its beauty and excite to the promise of great climbs as the top of the Esk Buttress first appears floating beneath the Scafells. People frequently ask which is my favourite mountain, place, walk, climb, etc. It is almost an impossible question to answer, for each day on the fells, on the mountains and in wild places is different and each has its own particular qualities. The pleasure in walking this route, however, and the longing for it, seems somehow stronger than all the rest.

RIGHT: The Heath Spotted Orchid is fairly common on Great Moss from June onwards. It is a spectacular flower, with purple line markings different on individual petals. Furthermore, in every colony each individual flower is unique both in its marking and its colour, which varies from very pale to deep purple.

OPPOSITE, TOP: Active in mid-June is the ferocious-looking Gold-Ringed Dragonfly, here shown in the bracken at the start of the walk up Mosedale. Strikingly marked, with huge green eyes, it is over 5cm in length. It darts at lightning speed and hovers effortlessly – let's hope it is harmless to humans!

OPPOSITE BELOW: A Large Tortoiseshell enjoys the sunshine on the flanks of Scafell Pike at an altitude of 488m.

BELOW: A wintery look from the head of Mosedale over Lingcove Beck (out of picture) and over Long Crag to Scafell Pike and Ill Crag. The climber's route to Great Moss, called by Jim Birkett the 'Falconer's Path', traverses beneath Long Crag but is unmarked on the Ordnance Survey map.

OPPOSITE: Beneath the col at the head of Mosedale runs the lively Lingcove Beck which must be crossed to gain the 'Falconer's Path' to Great Moss. Born high on the flanks of Bowfell, it proceeds over an impressive series of waterfalls before running beneath Lingcove Bridge to enter the River Esk. At the end of a hot day, there can be no finer experience in the mountains than taking a cooling plunge in Lingcove Beck.

BELOW: An intricately veined boulder rests on the edge of Great Moss. Despite first appearances, I am sure these are naturally formed and not the work of ancient man.

OPPOSITE: The final section of ascent from the end of Long Crag reveals this aspect of Cam Spout Crag over Great Moss; the summit of Scafell can be seen at the far right. Cam Spout Crag is a large cliff and there have been a number of climbs upon it, although the rock is not the best quality for climbing. It is the haunt of peregrine and raven and a precious habitat for mountain flora – I feel, even as a keen climber, that it is best left to nature. Originally this crag must have been known as Cam Crag: in Old Norse 'cam' means ridge, cams are the stones that top off Lakeland stone walls, and this is the shape of the crag. The waterfall to its side was accordingly named Cam Spout. The meaning of the original name must have been forgotten, for the crag was later renamed after the waterfall.

BELOW: *The very head of
Eskdale and the River Esk, seen
from Great Moss. Above and
beyond lies Esk Hause. Up the
sweeping slopes to the left (out
of picture) hangs the stark,
stone-filled hanging valley of
Little Narrowcove.*

BELOW: The regular path to the heights from Great Moss makes a rocky scramble just to the right of Cam Spout. It continues up the valley until just below the great bastion of the East Buttress, where the ways split. A scree-filled and bouldery rift to the left leads up to tiny Fox's Tarn and so to Scafell. Continuing straight on makes a steep ascent of scree direct to the ridge of Mickledore.

BELOW: Above the dog-leg of the River Esk, as it quits the end of Great Moss, and below the huge cliff of Cam Spout Crag, Sampson's Stones are draped around a little grassy hillock. Of considerable size, they give the impression of being arranged by man but are surely too big to have been moved by hand.

Coleridge was possibly the first person to describe them in a letter of 1802 to Sara Hutchinson: ' — & found that they were all huge stones'. Ruined stone walls and what appear to be manmade earthworks are to be found in the vicinity.

OPPOSITE: A detailed view of the lively Cam Spout, with the summit ridge of Scafell looking distinctively peak-like from this angle.

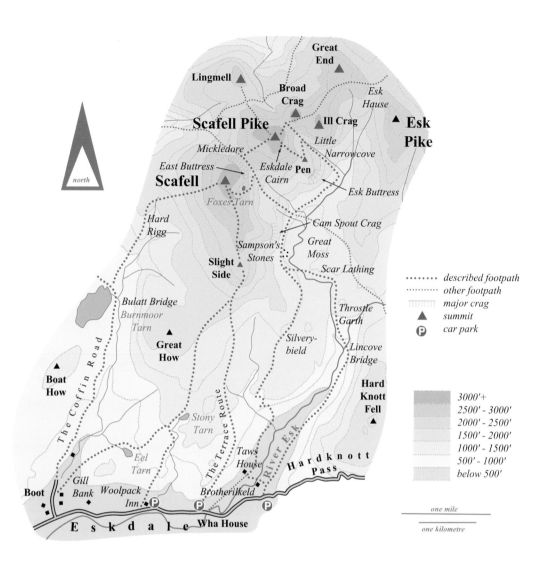

Great
End

Lingmell

Broad
Crag

Esk
Hause

Scafell Pike

Ill Crag

Esk
Pike

Mickledore

Little
Narrowcove

East Buttress

Eskdale
Cairn

Pen

Scafell

Esk Buttress

Foxes Tarn

Hard
Rigg

Cam Spout Crag

Sampson's
Stones

Great
Moss

Slight
Side

Scar Lathing

Bulatt Bridge

Burnmoor
Tarn

Throstle
Garth

**Great
How**

Silvery-
bield

Lincove
Bridge

**Boat
How**

The Coffin Road

**Hard
Knott
Fell**

Stony
Tarn

The Terrace Route

Eel
Tarn

Taws
House

River Esk

Boot

Gill
Bank

Woolpack
Inn

Brotherilkeld

Hardknott Pass

Eskdale Wha House

north

.... described footpath
.... other footpath
⊓⊓⊓⊓⊓ major crag
▲ summit
Ⓟ car park

3000'+
2500' - 3000'
2000' - 2500'
1500' - 2000'
1000' - 1500'
500' - 1000'
below 500'

one mile

one kilometre

Scafell
Slight Side

Scafell Pike

Broad Crag

Pen

Ill Crag

Great End

RIGHT AND OPPOSITE: This is arguably the finest aspect of the Scafells from the south, looking over Upper Eskdale from the summit of Harter Fell. On a bitterly cold day, the winter light emphasises the warm colours of rust-red bracken and orange-brown fell grass. Heavy snows arrived just days later.

This is the quieter side of the Scafells. Beyond the initial foothills these southern reaches offer a quite different perspective of the Massif: no Scafell enthusiast can pass them by.

THE APPROACHES FROM
ESKDALE

This is the quieter side of the the Scafells. There are many routes from the coarse, pink granite of Eskdale to all points of the Massif, all of them long and each with its own special solitude.

Brotherilkeld provides two excellent ways to approach the Great Moss and the wildness of Upper Eskdale. Either keep right of the River Esk (true left bank) to cross the packhorse stone arch of Lingcove Bridge and up Throstle Garth to pass beneath Scar Lathing to enter Great Moss on the west side of the river, or cross to Taw House and then make a zigzag ascent above Scale Bridge. This levels to cross the peat of Damas Dubs and through the enticing corridor of Silverybield Crag before emerging above Great Moss to cross by the boulders of Sampson's Stones below Cam Spout Crag.

Routes from Great Moss to all points of the Massif are many. To Scafell, the regular route ascends the spur right of Cam Spout waterfall and leads up the stony runnel valley towards the East Buttress of Scafell and Mickledore. The easiest ascent of Scafell from here, bearing left before the East Buttress, climbs via Fox's Tarn. An alternative is to follow the Cam Spout Ridge bearing off left above the waterfall. Direct routes up Scafell Pike involve walking along beneath the mighty, serenely beautiful sentinel rock of the Esk Buttress, until ascent can be made into Little Narrowcove. If this is continued, it emerges on to the neck of the col between Broad Crag (right) and Scafell Pike (left).

An airier route from the base of Little Narrowcove moves out left low down to gain the Eskdale Ridge, above the Esk Buttress, thereby ascending to the independent top of Pen. The ridge above leads via Rough Crag to Scafell Pike's Eskdale Cairn. If the Esk valley is followed in its entirety, then ascent leads to the high crossroads of Esk Hause.

Scafell is also popularly ascended via the Terrace Route from Wha House Farm. There is a small, rough car park just above the road opposite the farm; a stile over the fence starts the path. It proceeds to flank the hillside below Goat Crag and Bull How before cresting the fell and following along Cat Cove to make ascent of the broad shoulder to Slight Side. A different start to this route begins at the Woolpack Inn, further down the valley, to climb via Stony Tarn before joining the latter route up to Slight Side.

Don't forget your boots if you want to enjoy the different approaches from the hamlet of Boot. With the mountain of Scafell dominant, beyond the initial foothills these southern reaches offer a quite different perspective of the Massif: no Scafell enthusiast can pass them by.

The route via Gill Bank to Eel Tarn leads to a junction with the Woolpack path by Stony Tarn. Intriguing in its detail in the lower reaches, it opens beyond to reveal the great broad southern shoulder falling from Slight Side. This aspect is perhaps best viewed from the high road, from Eskdale to the Duddon, over Birker Fell or, alternatively, looking from the stone circles on the grassy heights of Burnmoor.

Last, though by no means least, there is the coffin road, leading from Boot to Wasdale Head across the flanks of Burnmoor beneath Eskdale Fell. This crosses the desolate Bulatt Bridge (not so much a bridge, more a plank of wood the last time I crossed) at the head of Burnmoor Tarn, then leads to the Hard Rigg shoulder route common with the ascent taken by Coleridge in 1802 (see Wasdale approaches).

OPPOSITE: This evocative view to Scafell over Brotherilkeld Farm just makes you want to get your boots on! The path beyond the buildings, running up the red-brackened fellside towards Slight Side, goes by Scale Gill waterfall. However, the classic route leading to Great Moss and offering a better position to traverse both Scafell Pike and Scafell passes Brotherilkeld Farm to ascend by the River Esk.

BELOW: Amazing light illuminates Scafell, seen from the Birker Fell road over Whincop Farm and Great Arming Crag. To the right are Esk Pike and Bowfell.

BELOW: Snows atop the Scafells over the white farmhouse of High Ground on Birker Fell. The flattish-topped fell in the middle ground, casting the shadow, is Great How on Eskdale Fell; above this is Slight Side, the south-western terminus of the Massif, then the summit of Scafell. The top peeking over the shoulder of Scafell is distant Kirkfell.

The final gathering of Herdwick sheep from the Scafells by Brotherilkeld Farm takes place late in the year, traditionally November. If the weather is bad, which is often the case, it is a highly skilled and physically demanding business, involving shepherds from different farms and many dogs operating as a team. They have to comb the rough ground from the summit plateau down for any strays.

OPPOSITE: Shepherd David Harrison of Brotherilkeld Farm and three border collies scour the hillside for stray Herdwicks, with the impressive Slight Side (locally named Horn Crag) behind.

ABOVE: Shepherds, dogs and sheep, soaked to the skin, are home at last and safely into the yard at Brotherilkeld Farm.

RIGHT: A recently clipped Herdwick ewe (called a shieling when it has been sheared for the first time), smit-marked with a distinctive red bar and returned to the fell. Standing defiantly on a rock, it stamped its hoof as I walked past. It knows its patch: Herdwicks are 'heathed' to a particular section of the fell, and as long as traditional methods of hill farming are maintained they will, with their lambs, always return to the same patch year in and year out.

BELOW: A walk on the wild side by the River Esk in Upper Eskdale – arguably the classic approach to the Scafells from Eskdale. The peak ahead is Bowfell.

OPPOSITE: Lingcove Bridge, Upper Eskdale. Ascent from this point leads above the ravine and waterfalls of the River Esk, on beneath the crag of Scar Lathing and into Great Moss beside Sampson's Stones. It is wonderful unspoilt country.

BELOW: Over Burnmoor Tarn to the top of Scafell. Bulatt Bridge, just a plank of wood at the time of writing, crosses Hardrigg Gill which is seen dropping from the upper reaches of the mountain. The shoulder of Hard Rigg, to the left of the gill, provides the most direct route to the summit of Scafell from Burnmoor Tarn. This is the route thought to have been followed by Coleridge in 1802.

OPPOSITE: Looking out from the Massif down from East Buttress over Cam Spout (out of picture, below) to Great Moss. Beyond to the left are the Crinkle Crags and beyond those lie the Southern Fells of Wetherlam, Grey Friar, Coniston Old Man and Dow Crag.

OVERLEAF: Looking from the Eskdale flanks of Scafell over Eel Tarn, Eskdale, Low Birker Tarn and Birker Fell to the distant blue heights of Blackcombe.

OPPOSITE: Looking north-north-east along the spine of the Massif from the summit dome of Scafell Pike, over a sunlit Broad Crag and on to the top of Great End.

THE SCAFELL MASSIF

The rooftop of England, the bony spine of the Scafells, is a great expanse of stone, boulder, scree and rocky knoll outcrops, with scarcely a blade of grass. Beneath two hulking ridges separated by the notch of Mickledore lie the greatest crags in England – along with hanging coves, tiny tarns, tumbling waterfalls and, far below, deep mountain valleys.

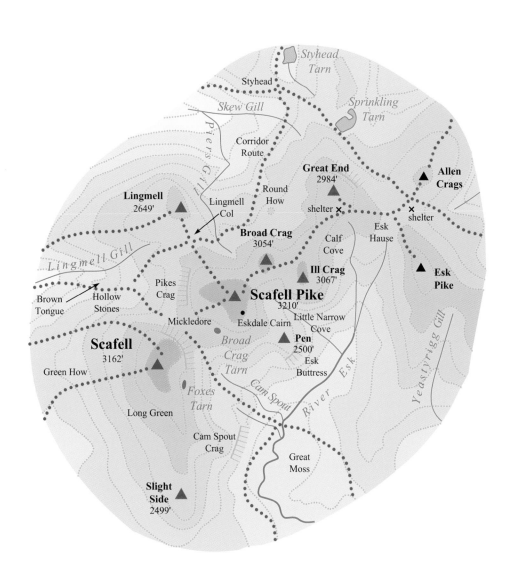

BELOW: Looking north to the
summit of Great End in the rosy
glow of the falling sun. In only a
few minutes, temperatures will
plummet to sub-zero levels.

BELOW: Heavy going: a lone figure approaches the north face of Great End through deep soft snow. I took this picture from the flanks of Allen Crags after making the long approach over Glaramara.

BELOW: From Westmorland Crags, looking over the head of Wasdale to Great Gable. On clear winter days such as this, even without snow, there are hazards for the unwary. Sections of the path may be covered in solid ice; what is normally loose and forgiving scree may have taken on the strength of unbreakable concrete, and once-forgiving grass slopes become as solid and slippery as brass.

BELOW: Snow-topped Great End, seen beyond Lingmell looking over the very head of Wasdale. Despite a brief burst of sunshine, nicely illuminating the fresh snow, the leaden sky indicates that more snow is on the way.

OVERLEAF: Great End Crag in summer looks benign and markedly less serious than when clad in snow and ice. Its generous mantle of foliage shows that in general its angle is some way off the vertical. Central Gully and, to its left, South East Gully are prominent. I was once winter climbing here with ice axes, crampons and rope, on what felt like fairly steep ground, when a red fox jogged past, making a horizontal traverse of the cliff look like a walk in the park!

OPPOSITE, TOP: To the head of Eskdale and Esk Hause, with the Ill Crag tops to the left. The right-hand separate rock bluff looks to be set lower from this angle. The rocks of Esk Pike, falling to Esk Hause, are on the right and are distinctly lighter in colour than those of the Scafell Massif. Locally, for reasons made obvious from this angle, Ill Crag is nicknamed Camel's Humps. The rocky knoll down to the right, left of the source of the River Esk, is known as Cockley Pike.

OPPOSITE, BELOW: Naked rock predominates in this view from the top of Pen, looking north over the remote and seldom-visited Little Narrowcove. The summit of Ill Crag stands top right, with its lesser second top distinct to the right. Beneath Ill Crag, a grassy diagonal break climbs up to the right: this is the interestingly named Yorkshire Rake – a little bit of Yorkshire in the heart of Cumbria, the cheek of it! Top left, forming the head of this steep cove of sweeping scree, is Green Crag, the Eskdale face of Broad Crag whose summit can be seen above.

BELOW: With the moon already up, I had better get a move on if I am to walk back to Langdale tonight. Looking from the top of Ill Crag west to Esk Pike and Bowfell, the wonderfully coloured rocky bluff second top of Ill Crag is in the foreground to the left of the image.

OPPOSITE: To the rock-strewn top of Ill Crag, with Esk Pike beyond, looking from the Eskdale Cairn on Scafell Pike. It is an inhospitable, secluded and little-trod area of the Massif – and long may it remain so.

ABOVE: View south-west to Broad Crag, a distinct rocky dome protected by crags and steep places in a shot taken from a little way below the main spine on the Wasdale side of the Massif.

LEFT: The considerable dome of Broad Crag, seen from the Corridor Route on the Wasdale side of the mountain. For those walking the spine of the Massif, this is not a place to stray off the path. For the sake of safety, it is probably a good thing that relatively few walkers ever visit the summit of Broad Crag: the main path cuts beneath it, on the Eskdale side, on its dash to Scafell Pike.

RIGHT: At the day's end, with the moon rising, a climber makes his return from Scafell over Broad Crag.

OVERLEAF: Silhouetted against a purple sky, as the evening quiet gathers, the black slopes of Broad Crag swoop down towards the head of Wasdale.

Tiny Broadcrag Tarn nestles below Eskdale Cairn on Scafell Pike. It is the highest tarn in the Lake District at approximately 830m, some 4m higher than Fox's Tarn, located opposite on the flanks of Scafell.

OPPOSITE: Looking over the tarn in the direction of Eskdale.

BELOW: Looking in the opposite direction, out to Scafell's East Buttress and Mickledore.

LEFT: The summit trig point, facing west, with rime ice fingers growing in the direction of the prevailing wind. Behind the edge of the summit dome is a small snippet of a wonderful vista: Kirkfell, Grasmoor and the distant Scottish hills on the other side of the Solway Firth.

BELOW: Looking north-north-west from the summit of Scafell Pike. In the near foreground can be seen the top of Lingmell; beyond are arrayed the local Wasdale fells, with Great Gable to the right, Kirkfell in the centre and Pillar to the left.

BELOW: Snow-clad Mickledore, the ridge/arête separating Scafell Pike (left) from Scafell (right), is seen from beneath Scafell Crag on the Wasdale side. The white cloud over on Scafell Pike is spindrift – clouds of ice particles, picked up and blown by the strong prevailing winds. Despite the blue sky, conditions feel arctic due to the wind chill. In the lee of the wind, deposits of unstable, unconsolidated blown snow accumulate, creating the risk of avalanche.

RIGHT: A Neolithic stone axe found on Scafell Pike. Probably buried in peat for thousands of years, its tuff surface has been denatured and oxidised by the acidic environment, which has changed its colour from a natural steely grey-blue to this ghostly white.

RIGHT: This neat little basin-like hollow in a larger boulder field is an axe chipping point, possibly some six thousand years old. Sadly, quite large areas of this important site have been damaged by over-enthusiastic amateur archaeologists.

OPPOSITE: Upright stones on the Eskdale slopes of Eskdale Cairn, near the summit of Scafell Pike. Are they a natural occurrence or arranged by man?

ABOVE: To my eye there is as much form, fascination and beauty in these volcanic rocks and outcrops scattered around the Scafells than in many man-made objects of art.

BELOW: Looking south from the summit plateau of Scafell Pike over the Eskdale Cairn. Harter Fell is the mountain to the left, and the tiny cone of Stickle Pike can be seen before the flats of Duddon Sands. The hill at the distant right is Blackcombe. Though at first it may look like a man-made collection of stones, the Eskdale Cairn is a natural rock outcrop with only a small man-made cairn on the top.

OPPOSITE: Looking from the Eskdale Cairn, the Scafell Pike summit cairn marks the highest point in England.

OVERLEAF: Looking by Pikes Crag, over the flanks of Lingmell, to Mosedale and Pillar mountain in the background. Pikes Crag tends to be forgotten due to its imposing near neighbours, Scafell Crags and the East Buttress just over the crest of Mickledore. This is a shame, as it is an excellent rock, some 76m in vertical height, which gets a good dose of summer sunshine. My late great friend Bill Peascod climbed his only new route on the Scafells here – the classic Wriggling Route (it does not wriggle at all, in fact, but climbs the central arête of the crag direct).

BELOW: The roof of England: bare rock, in the form of scattered scree and broken crags, dominates this image of the summit plateau of Scafell Pike, taken from Scafell. The summit cairn is in the centre and the Eskdale Cairn to the right. The curving path sweeping in and out again from the left is the one rising from Mickledore. The observant will notice the tiny tarnlet of Broadcrag Tarn in the bottom right third of the image.

BELOW: North-west from Pike de Bield with the Eskdale Cairn of Scafell Pike at the top left and, to the right, looking over Little Narrowcove, Broad Crag and Ill Crag. The huge cliff is the Esk Buttress (more properly known as Dow Crag), one of the finest rock climbing crags in the region.

LEFT: The original masonry of this building is neat and coursed, it boasts a stone hearth and lintel, a stone-flagged floor and a raised stone bench around the inside. It may have been built as a shelter by early nineteenth-century surveyors doing their first triangulations, or perhaps it was a tea house serving the new tourists streaming to the summit of England's mountain. Whatever its origins, although only about 100m from the busy summit cairn it is seldom noticed today.

BELOW: The numerous ruined walls and structures are not immediately obvious among the rocks and boulders spread across the entire summit dome of Scafell Pike. Certainly, some are modern and have been built as day or bivouac shelters by groups or schools. Others appear to be much older, and resemble the remains of hut circles from prehistoric times. This view from the summit cairn looking out towards Bowfell and the Crinkle Crags shows a couple of rough rectangular enclosures, probably of fairly recent construction, followed by a much neater coursed building.

OPPOSITE: To Scafell Pike, beyond Ill Crag, looking from Esk Pike. Clouds gather around the ridge falling from the Eskdale Cairn to Pen as rain sweeps down Little Narrowcove.

OVERLEAF: Tiny figures on the summit cairn of Scafell Pike, viewed from the flanks of Broad Crag, stand silhouetted against the night sky. The bump on the left is the Eskdale Cairn.

BELOW: Down the ridge, falling from Rough Crag to the top of Pen, with clouds rising from Eskdale's Great Moss below.

RIGHT: Seen from Ill Crag, the independent nature of little Pen is clear. Great Moss, drained by the young River Esk, lies below.

BELOW: Snow clings to the steeps of Lingmell with the clouds gathering around the heights of Scafell Pike to the left and Scafell to the right.

OVERLEAF: A quick burst of sunshine generates a rainbow among the squally showers blasting down Wasdale. This is a view to Lingmell, across Wasdale Head from Yewbarrow.

BELOW: An ice fringe adorns the East Buttress.

OPPOSITE: Rapidly melting icicles hang free from the overhanging rocks of the East Buttress.

BELOW: West to the sun setting behind Scafell Crag and the rocky knoll top of Deep Ghyll Buttress. Many people ask me how I get home once darkness falls on the tops. My official answer is that I always carry a head torch; those with first-hand knowledge know that a more accurate answer would be by moonlight and the seat of my pants!

OPPOSITE: With the notch and spike marking the passage of Lord's Rake at the top left, the profiled flanks of Shamrock fall for another 100m into Hollow Stones.

BELOW: The cairned rocky knoll top of Deep Ghyll Buttress provides a dominant high point above the great horseshoe of cliffs that form the north-eastern terminus of Scafell. Seen beyond, to the left of the cairn, are Scafell Pike and the Eskdale Cairn.

RIGHT: Over Deep Ghyll to the summit of Deep Ghyll Buttress (marked as Symonds Knott on the 1:25,000 Ordnance Survey map). Is it a contender to be classed as a top in its own right? Deep Ghyll provides a good link with the West Wall Traverse and so down to Lord's Rake. It could be classed as a steep scrambly walk in summer conditions; in winter the difficulty varies enormously, though as a general rule it should be regarded as a climb rather than a walk.

LEFT: Looking out from Fox's Tarn toward Scafell Pike. Set a little lower than Broadcrag Tarn, it surely makes the record books for being the smallest 'official' tarn. With its own borran of boulders, spring and tiny stream outlet, it forms a little oasis of green among the grey rock. It is certainly one of the loveliest of high mountain places.

BELOW: A large black beetle by the side of Fox's Tarn does its best not to be photographed.

BELOW: The hanging cove left of the East Buttress is occupied by Fox's Tarn, with the summit of Scafell above and just a little to the right. Although Fox's Tarn is technically the easiest of the routes from the Scafell Pike side up Scafell, it is not the pleasantest in execution. The rift dropping from the basin, seen here, is the line of ascent. In effect, it is a stream bed with loose rocks of all sizes. Above the tarn, unstable scree, trending diagonally rightwards, has to be climbed, and the stone steps laid in the 1980s have unfortunately become loose and, in some cases, have slid away.

BELOW: The plunging and
grossly overhanging nature of
the East Buttress is seen to good
effect in this image. Since the
1930s, this crag has proved a
testing ground for many of
Britain's finest climbers; the
routes here are among the
hardest in Britain.

BELOW: Scafell Crag in thick snow: I saw it like this on a number of occasions in the 1980s, but never since. On this day we walked from Borrowdale to climb Steep Ghyll, which was then rated as one of the hardest winter climbs on the Scafells. And yes, despite a liberal filling of snow, it was steep.

BELOW: A winter view towards Hollow Stones from the path traversing from Lingmell Col to beneath Pikes Crag. The great steep blackness just right of centre is Scafell Shamrock. The notch in the skyline is the rent of Deep Ghyll separating the rocks on the right from the immensity of Scafell Crag to its left (much foreshortened in this image).

LEFT: A lone figure, my climbing companion and friend of long standing Rick Graham, is dwarfed approaching the fearsome East Buttress. This is a colour photograph, but on that day black and white were the predominant colours. We were looking for icicles to climb. If we had found one long and large enough, and if we had managed to climb it, we would have achieved the first winter ascent of the East Buttress.

BELOW: On the Eskdale side of Scafell, the East Buttress is seen top right in this view over Great Moss – even from this distance it looks seriously challenging. It was at this point, on our way to look at peregrines on Cam Spout, that my father informed me that it was the most formidable climbing crag in Britain. The nearer dominant crag is Cam Spout, with the waterfall to its right. The top on the skyline at the left is Long Green and just right of centre is the summit of Scafell.

OPPOSITE: Seen from Scafell Pike, the adjoining ridge of Mickledore abuts the great horseshoe of cliffs that run around the hulking form of Scafell. With the East Buttress to the left and Scafell Crag to the right, there is no easy direct route between the two Scafells. Above the ramparts stands the distinctive rocky knoll that forms the top of Deep Ghyll Buttress, while the summit of the mountain lies along the shoulder to its left. Below and beyond we see Wast Water, then the towers of the Sellafield nuclear plant and finally, over the sea, the faint outline of the Isle of Man. The great poet Norman Nicholson, from nearby Millom, summed up many people's feelings about the nuclear plant in his powerful poem 'Windscale' (1972):
'Scafell looks down from the bracken band,
'And sees hell in a grain of sand.'

LEFT: From the depths of Moss Ghyll, this awful mechanically constructed track runs from Hollow Stones to Lingmell Col. A digger was flown up in sections by helicopter and reassembled to carry out its destructive work. In my opinion there is no place for such a symmetrical switchback track among the wilds of the Lakeland Fells. It looks artificial and alien; conservationists refer to this sort of thing as 'creeping urbanisation'. Has the Lake District National Park Authority no longer eyes to see?

BELOW: Looking from the top of Deep Ghyll Buttress in the direction of Scafell summit, the cross in the col below serves as a useful pointer in poor visibility. From this angle, the head of the cross points to Fox's Tarn, the tail to the top of the Green How route, the nearest arm to Deep Ghyll and the far arm to the summit of Scafell.

BELOW: Looking down to
Burnmoor Tarn from the summit
shoulder of Scafell. The tarn
issues into the silvery beck
seen to the left, Whillan Beck,
and not down the valley of
Miterdale which runs in line
with it. Beyond the foot of
Miterdale is the low outline
of Muncaster Fell and then
the West Coast by the Roman
port of Ravenglass.

OPPOSITE: A magnificent
sunset is reflected in the ice-
skinned snows of Esk Pike, with
the shoulder of Scafell dropping
to Slight Side silhouetted
beyond. It looks warm, but I
can assure you it most certainly
was not!

BELOW: The upturned nose
of Slight Side marks the south-
western terminus of the Scafells.
This view looks over Upper
Eskdale and High Scarth from
Little Stand.

OVERLEAF: The broad ridge
that drops from Scafell over
Long Green and finally to Slight
Side, with Harter Fell on the far
side of Eskdale beyond. Only a
couple of hours now before I
am home and able to put my
feet up.

CLIMBING SCAFELL: A SHORT HISTORY

INTRODUCTION

The cliffs of Scafell offer some of the toughest, longest, most remote and highest mountain climbs in Britain. From the verticality of Scafell Crags, through the sun-kissed pillar of Esk Buttress, the delights of little Pikes Crag and the massively overhanging barrel-shaped profile of the East Buttress to the snow-plastered expanse of Great End, the long history and intensity of climbing here are exceptional. Generations of climbers, pitting their skill and daring, have pushed the limits of what was previously thought possible – with triumphs and tragedies, good days and bad days, heroes and villains.

Climbing on the Scafells consists of both rock climbing and winter mountaineering, the use of finger and toe as well as ice axe and crampon, the ascent of technical rock and snow and ice. From tentative beginnings, with no specialist equipment or safeguards nor knowledge of what was possible, climbers have reached the present-day world of the specialist rock athlete, who can ascend incredibly overhanging rock using impossibly tiny holds and highly developed equipment and technique. It is my opinion that, with the same level of knowledge and equipment, there would be little difference between the greats of each generation. O. G. Jones, high on Scafell Pinnacle with nailed boots and no safeguards, or Dave Birkett, scaling the East Buttress with friction-grip rock-climbing shoes and chalked hands – both have pushed beyond known limits at the cutting edge of mental and physical performance.

The majority of climbers just do what they love best, whether a sunny amble up Pikes Crag or a more challenging climb up one of the magnificent classic routes – theirs is also the story of Scafell climbing. The real key to success is self-fulfilment and quality of route; a wise climber sets his or her own limits and pitches ability accordingly. The bottom line is personal enjoyment, and for each individual the fascination, passion and attraction of climbing are different.

However, it would be misguided to think of climbing on the Scafells merely as an athletic sport. The climbing here is remote and it is serious; usually the rock is slightly damp or wears a thin cloak of moss or lichen. Even with the latest equipment, many routes are poorly protected. To climb here successfully requires a degree of commitment – for many it becomes an all-consuming passion.

As I write this history of climbing on the Scafells, I cannot help noting that both the first and the last recorded rock climbs on the East Buttress were made by Lakeland-based Birketts. The first climb was made via Broad Stand by Edward Birkett of Keswick on 7 June 1815, accompanied by Jonathan Otley. The last was Return of the King, made by Dave Birkett of Langdale on 4 June 2006. Between lie some two hundred years of history: a fascinating story of the greatest and most colourful characters ever to participate in the great game of climbing.

1800 to 1880: TINY ACORNS

It is not certain which ways through the Scafell Crags were known about and used in times past, but early written records are based around the route now known as Broad Stand which, in climbing terminology, is regarded as of moderate difficulty. Today, Broad Stand is generally used by climbers as a convenient and easy descent from the East Buttress or Scafell Crags, but for non-climbers, hillwalkers or runners, it remains a dauntingly exposed and challenging way of ascending from Mickledore directly to the summit shoulder of Scafell Pike.

Focus on Broad Stand began on 5 August 1802, when the poet Samuel Taylor Coleridge descended the cliffs of Scafell directly to Mickledore. He was out on a nine-day solo walking tour of the western Lakes when, with scant detailed knowledge, he decided to gain the valley of Eskdale directly from the summit of Scafell. Whether it was inexperience, incompetence or bravado – or a mixture of all three – it was a radical and daring thing to do, and encapsulates the free spirit, sense of adventure and unconventionality that are the very essence of climbing.

Prior to ascending Scafell, he lodged with Thomas Tyson of Wasdale Head. Tyson filled in some details of the complex topography and this, together with a brief mention of Scafell in William Hutchinson's *History of Cumberland*, was all the information he had on the Massif. From the summit, suitably impressed with the view and position, Coleridge wrote:

> But O! what a look down under my Feet! The frightfullest Cove that might ever be seen? huge perpendicular Precipices, and one Sheep upon its only Ledge, that surely must be a crag! Tyson told me of this place, & called it Hollow Stones. Just by it & joining together, rise two huge Pillars of bare lead-coloured stone – / but their height & depth is terrible. – I must now drop down, how I may into Eskdale – that lies under to my right – the upper part of it wildest and savagest surely of all the Vales that were ever seen from the Top of an English Mountain / and the lower part the loveliest.

OPPOSITE: *George Abraham climbs the narrow ridge to the top of Scafell Pinnacle, assisted by Gaspard, a professional French mountain guide who was hired by the Wastwater Hotel in the years before 1914.*

The next part of his letter, containing a riveting account of his subsequent descent, was written from the farm of Toes in Eskdale, now known as Taw House, farmed by his host John Towers. It portrays a graphic account of how he gripped and hung from his arms, letting go and dropping from ledge to ledge, fighting the fear of continuing since he had no way of going back, until he finally reached the distinctive 'rent' at the bottom (see page 22). It is a description many climbers who have pushed themselves to the limit will recognise. I find the following particularly poignant:

> When the Reason & the Will are away, what remain to us but Darkness & Dimness and a bewildering Shame, and pain that is utterly Lord over us, or fantastic Pleasure, that draws the Soul along swimming through the air in many shapes, even as a Flight of Starlings in a Wind.

Coleridge's exploits on Broad Stand certainly influenced Thomas Tyson and John Towers: surely, if a poet and romantic could penetrate the defences of Scafell, couldn't they? This precedent, and the knowledge that tourism was increasing, must have been a considerable motivation for them to establish such routes, and the two local men went on to probe the weaknesses of the Wasdale side of Scafell Crag.

The catalyst to explore further and record proven routes was provided by the Ambleside artist William Green, and Jonathan Otley from Keswick. Green published his *Guide to the Lakes* in two illustrated volumes in 1818–19; part guide and part travelogue, it was intended specifically for 'tourists'. Otley, an important figure in opening up the Lakes, provided the accompanying map. Green's description of the Scafells includes the following:

> On the 7th of June, 1815, Mr Otley, with Mr Edward Birkett, guide and fisherman, left Keswick at five in the morning, and having breakfasted at Rosthwaite, journied to Seathwaite, from which they then ascended to Sty Head, and Sprinkling Tarns, gaining the High Man by the way just described. From the High Man Mr Otley and I descended, and at the end of half a mile, winding among and over large stones, came to Mickle Door. The footing at this door is grassy, and its middle a sharp ridge, from which, through immense rocks, is an opening on the south west to Wastdale Head; and on the south east over the heads of Eskdale, and Seathwaite, to the Coniston mountains, on either hand grand, romantic, and awfully interesting.
>
> The Crags on the south west, though seeming frightfully to oppose all passage, have been ascended as the readiest way to the top of Scafell, and among other adventurers by Mr Thomas Tyson, of Wastdale Head, and Mr Towers, of Toes: but Messrs. Otley, and Birkett, contented themselves by proceeding for some distance, in the direction of Eskdale, to a deep fissure, through which they scrambled to the top of Scafell, and thence descended to Wasdale Head, a decent days march for a man like Birkett, then 66 years of age . . .

Although it has been suggested that the 'deep fissure' could have been the great rift of Mickledore Chimney, further down towards Eskdale and flanking the edge of the East Buttress, I have no doubt that Green's description fits an ascent of Broad Stand: the first recorded rock climb in Britain. Birkett and Otley ascended Broad Stand, while Tyson and Towers had already ascended Lord's Rake, and possibly Deep Ghyll via the West Wall Traverse.

1880s to 1899: GREAT OAKS

To a Wasdale scene of explorers and hillwalkers, buzzing with energy born of the freedom of the mountains, a new dimension was soon added. The chief early protagonist, later known as 'the father of rock climbing', was W. P. Haskett Smith, Old Etonian, Oxford graduate and free thinker. He developed the philosophy that it was perfectly acceptable, even highly desirable, to climb something just for the fun of it – reaching the summit of a mountain was, for him, a secondary consideration. Photographs of him in later life portray a 'Wild Bill Hickock'-looking character, with great drooping moustache, impish smile and twinkling eyes. During the 1880s he began recording rock climbs for their own sake. He made a number of first ascents up the gullies around the mighty Scafell Pinnacle, and launched out on 20 September 1884 to climb the exposed knife-edge arête leading up from Scafell Pinnacle's Low Man to the isolated summit of High Man, before crossing Jordan Gap between to the separate pinnacle top of Pisgah Buttress. These are the two distinct pinnacles that can be seen from the summit plateau near the top of Deep Ghyll. Haskett Smith's greatest single achievement was the solo ascent in 1886 of the 24m pinnacle of rock on Great Gable known as Napes Needle, 'without ropes or other illegitimate means'. Bold, imaginative, brilliant: the ascent of this evocative and shapely finger of rock inspired a new breed of climbers.

Up to this point, mountaineering had been considered a game for members of the privileged classes, who had played a major part in developments in the European Alps and greater mountains further afield. At variance with this image of climbing as a 'non-competitive sport', numerous individuals and groups were now in contention for honours, and virtually the whole of the Scafells lay open to them. A party led by Norman Collie succeeded in ascending the mighty Moss Ghyll from bottom to top a couple of days after Christmas in 1892. Whether this ascent falls into the category of rock climbing or winter mountaineering is difficult to judge – it would depend on how much snow and ice prevailed. Collie succeeded because, as he admitted, he used an ice axe to cut a foothold on the crux of the climb; to this day that section of the route is known as 'Collie's Step'.

Outrage ensued, with the establishment making huge play that cutting steps in rock was unacceptable and that 'artificial aids' should never be used in British rock climbing. Similar controversies have continued at regular intervals throughout the history of climbing. The rules are constantly shifting; in most cases it is the status of the 'offender' within the climbing community at the time that dictates exactly who or what is controversial. Norman Collie was an exceptional mountaineer and an accomplished rock climber; I believe he fuelled the debate for his own amusement. All he did was

ABOVE: Bob Wightman on the final wall, Collie's Exit, of Moss Ghyll.

Collie's ascent opened the floodgates; within a few days Moss Ghyll received two further ascents – one by J. Collier and party, who added a direct and difficult finish seldom climbed today, and one solo by the bespectacled schoolmaster O. G. (the 'Only Genuine') Jones, who shot across the climbing and mountaineering scene as the brightest meteor of his generation, leaving a legacy of breathtaking climbs. He fell from Collie's Step and was saved only by an ingenious self-belaying rope technique that was years ahead of the time; after the fall, he continued to complete the climb with two broken ribs. Jones moved climbing from the confines and relative security of the gullies out on to open and exposed faces. On Scafell, he notably made ascents of the front faces of the two huge pillars right of the Central Buttress in 1898. On Scafell Pinnacle, Jones's Route Direct from Lord's Rake was climbed with G. T. Walker and, most significantly, he climbed Pisgah Buttress with the Abraham brothers. In 1899, Jones was pulled to his death by a falling guide on the iced ridge of the Dent Blanche in the Swiss Alps.

The Abraham brothers, George and Ashley, were photographers from Keswick; their pairing with O. G. Jones not only produced noteworthy climbs but resulted in an outstanding classic of mountaineering literature, perhaps the most influential book ever produced on Lakeland rock climbing. *Rock Climbing in the English Lake District* was written by Jones, illustrated by the Abrahams' photographs and published by G. P. Abraham & Sons in 1897.

Noteworthy of this early period was the first recorded ascent of Mickledore Chimney made by C. W. Dymond on 12 September 1893.

1900 to 1930: A NEW CENTURY

The Abraham brothers went on to produce numerous books on climbing and mountaineering, all wonderfully illustrated with original photographs. These books marketed and popularised climbing, opening the beauty and grandeur of the mountains to a wider audience. The brothers were at the forefront of the founding of the Fell and Rock Climbing Club in 1906.

At the beginning of the new century, the majority of climbers were under the impression that no further routes could be found on the Scafell Crags! It seemed beyond their reach to repeat Jones's achievements, let alone to contemplate the huge vertical blank spaces that remained. A modest, self-effacing Yorkshireman called Fred Botterill was to prove them all wrong. A genius on rock, he was the first of many to make their mark on Lakeland climbing who cut their teeth on gritstone edges – rounded, steep and rough, grit provides a superb medium on which to hone strength and technique.

Left of the central face of Scafell Crag, on a protruding buttress at right angles to the run of the face, a great raking slab caught Botterill's eye. He wrote in the 1903 Yorkshire Ramblers' Club journal:

> The idea of a new climb of any importance in the Wasdale district had never crossed our minds, and the suggestion of one on Scafell Crags – perhaps the most frequented rocks of all – would, if proposed, have been received with derision.

prize away a loose flake of rock – no more nor less than his contemporaries did, or the thousands of climbers since who have followed up deep, dank gullies. Collie was responsible for early pioneering in the Canadian Rockies and even attempted to climb the Himalayan giant Nanga Parbat. His rock climbing exploits, particularly in Scotland and the Black Cuillin of Skye, are also impressive.

A research scientist at University College London, Collie was no stranger to controversy. As an after-dinner speaker he would evoke the ghost story of the 'Old Grey Man' of Ben Macdui. He also claimed to be the first to take an X-ray photograph and to construct a neon lamp, claims that are somewhat at variance with the official scientific history of the period. As for his sighting of the 'Old Grey Man', who is to say whether it was true or not?

Botterill probably never really appreciated how good he was – climbing seemed easy to him, his associates describing his style as effortless. Leading the 30m slab in nailed boots, with no protection, at a technical grade harder than anything done before, he cleaned away moss and a bird's nest (probably that of a raven) with his bare fingers as he climbed, and dropped his ice axe. On completing the last few difficult moves, he wrote:

> This was sensational but perfectly safe. As usual I started with the wrong foot, and after taking two steps was obliged to go back. The next time I started with the left foot, then came the right, again the left, and lastly a long stride with the right brought me into the chimney.

And so, on 2 June 1903, quietly and without fuss, he completed the first ascent of the eponymous Botterill's Slab, then the hardest rock climb on the Scafells.

Stark reality returned later that year. On 21 September, with a strong wind blowing, a party of four competent and experienced climbers set off to tackle the Scafell Pinnacle, probably by Jones's 1898 route which still had not

ABOVE: A cross at the foot of Scafell Pinnacle commemorates the accident of 21 September 1903 when four climbers plunged to their deaths. The initials below the left arm are WB, WG, SR and HJ.

BELOW: Climbers on Botterill's Slab on Scafell Crag, first ascended on 2 June 1903 by Fred Botterill.

received a second ascent. Protection was non-existent and belays scarce when the lead climber fell. R. W. Broadrick, the most competent and experienced of the group, had been climbing but was thought to have handed over the lead to A. E. W. Garrett. Garrett apparently slipped, pulling the others to their deaths at the foot of the Pinnacle; a cross chipped into the rock commemorates the tragedy. Further development was stifled for almost a decade.

Siegfried Herford and George Sansom were under-graduates, both mad keen on rock climbing, both extremely fit, both to develop a particular love for the mountains around Wasdale Head. They formed one of the strongest climbing partnerships ever forged on British rock. Herford had the edge, but Sansom was also a very fine climber. In 1912 they repeated Jones's route up the Pinnacle Face and ascended Botterill's Slab, finding no particular difficulty in either. They also added a more direct route on the Pinnacle Face, known as Direct to Hopkinson's Cairn, as well as completing a girdle traverse covering the breadth of the Scafell Crags.

Years later, in *Climbing at Wasdale before the First World War* (Castle Cary Press, 1982), Sansom wrote of Herford:

> He was tall, slim, and graceful in movement, and when I read Kipling's description of Kamal's son 'That dropped from a mountain crest – he trod the ling like a buck in Spring and looked like a lance at rest', I felt that was a suitable description for S. W. Herford.

Despite all that had been done so far, the highest section of the Scafell Crags, the Central Buttress, still stood impregnable. It was beyond contemplation as a climb, consisting of 60m of plumb vertical rock with no apparent breaks or weaknesses. However, during explorations for the Girdle Traverse, Herford and Sansom discovered that on this apparently blank buttress, the Great Flake, a huge shield of rock exfoliating from the blank vertical mass, presented some kind of opportunity. As T. H. Lawrence wrote in his *Seven Pillars of Wisdom*:

> All men dream; but not equally. Those who dream by night in the dusty recesses of their minds awake to find that it was vanity; but the dreamers of day are dangerous men. That they may act their dreams with open eyes to make it possible.

Herford and Sansom dared to dream. Sansom wrote (in his article 'Central Buttress', 1914):

> It was not until June 1913 that we had the opportunity of putting this theory into practice on the Central Buttress. It is, however, one thing to talk lightheartedly of trying to climb a narrow 40ft crack of which the top overhangs the bottom by some 12ft, and quite another thing to stand at its foot prepared to do so.

But they were hooked, and made multiple attempts. Finally, using combined tactics on the chockstone, they succeeded on 20 April 1914. This first ascent of the Central Buttress of Scafell is regarded as a major breakthrough in climbing standards, and is possibly Britain's most famous route: whole books have been written about it. The terrible waste of

World War I ensured that many climbers who had shaped developments never saw their beloved fells again; Siegfried Herford was one of the many to perish.

Yet others began to fill the vacuum as early as the start of the 1920s, and an unprecedented wave of development began. Attitudes and techniques changed rapidly; many more people began to climb and standards increased. Riding the crest of this wave – approaching the climbing scene afresh with new techniques, rope management and practical, factual guidebooks – was Harry Kelly. He revolutionised rock climbing by popularising the use of 'rubbers', as opposed to nailed boots or stockinged feet. These were plimsolls (pumps) with a soft rubber sole, which give tremendous grip in dry conditions, enabling the climber to use friction holds that were impossible with nailed boots. Glaringly obvious now, it shocked the establishment to the core when Kelly declared in 1915:

> It is much more difficult climbing in nailed boots than rubbers especially where holds are small and also necessitate high reach up of the foot.

Indeed, such was the controversy that some climbers were still heatedly debating this issue when I started climbing in the 1960s!

Kelly was a modern thinker: he believed that women should be recognised as climbers in their own right – something that is taken for granted today, but at the time was a sensational concept. And he practised what he preached. He actively encouraged his wife Emily, a tremendous climber who had already soloed Jones's route on the Pinnacle Face, to found the Pinnacle Club in 1921, a climbing club solely for women. With Mrs Blanche Eden-Smith, he climbed one of the best routes ever on Scafell Crags, the exposed run of tapering slab bounding the right wall of Central Buttress, the delectable Moss Ghyll grooves. Kelly lifted climbing on Scafell out of one era and moved it on to the next.

1930 to 1950: THE GOOD OLD BOYS OF THE CLIMBERS' CLUB AND THE LOCAL HERO

The future of climbing on the Scafells now lay on the overhanging, uncompromising East Buttress and the great vertical bastion of Esk Buttress. Prior to World War II there were a number of key players, only a few of whom I have space to detail here. Liverpool-based Colin Kirkus had already achieved great things on Wales's mightiest mountain cliff, Clogwyn du' Arddu, high on the west flank of Snowdon. On Scafell he kicked off with the delicate and bold Mickledore grooves in May 1931, an outstanding flanking route. Quiet and modest, Kirkus was a wonderful climber with a discerning eye for a line.

The next new route, the Great Eastern, climbed on 21 August 1932, tackling the overhanging East Buttress head on at its central point, was to prove one of the greatest climbs on the crag. Remarkably, despite its zigzag course through the overhanging mass by a series of corners and hanging slabs, the technical difficulty of the Great Eastern is relatively low, a surprising quality that makes it very special. But Maurice Linnell, at the top of his powers, and a young novice called Sid Cross would not have known this – and it must have seemed a formidable undertaking. The night before, Linnell

picked up Sid with his motorbike and sidecar from a school rugby game in Kendal, and they had driven on to Wasdale Head before ascending to Mickledore. Here they spent the night out on the mountain, waiting for dawn. I once asked Sid what his feelings were, faced with the virgin overhanging mass of East Buttress on that summer's morn. His typically understated reply suggested that he felt it was nothing out of the ordinary!

The following year Linnell went on to climb another three formidable new routes on the East Buttress: Overhanging Wall on 23 July 1933, with A. T. Hargreaves and one peg aid; Morning Wall on 13 August 1933 with A. T. Hargreaves and W. Clegg (plus aid); Yellow Slab on 10 September 1933, with H. Pearson and one peg aid. He was pushing into the next grade of difficulty and found it necessary to use artificial aid on all three climbs; on two of them this took the form of a piton (peg) hammered into the rock. Many felt the piton was out of place on British crags and should not be used; however, Linnell was undeniably the man of the moment, and he wrote of his aid point on Overhanging Wall:

ABOVE: Siegfried Herford re-enacts for the camera his first ascent, with George Sansom, of the Great Flake of Central Buttress in April 1914; he is protected in this instance by a top-rope from H. C. Bowen.

fine climbs and a book that proved an inspiration to many, *Let's Go Climbing* (1941).

When quarryman Jim Birkett burst on the scene with his ascent of the East Buttress on 1 May 1938 (May Day Climb), it was considerably harder than anything done before. No aid was used, although three home-made pitons were used for security: two for belays, and a third for a running belay. Over the next decade, Jim climbed some eighteen new routes on the Scafells, developing possibilities on all three of its major cliffs: the East Buttress, Esk Buttress and Scafell Crags.

1950s: ROUGH AND TUMBLE

The end of the war energised and mobilised a whole social group that hitherto had effectively been denied access to the crags. These were the irreverent, liberated, boisterous, inner-city working class. Their modes of transport were the BSA, AJS, Matchless and Triumph. Groups included the Bradford Lads and the Rock and Ice. They were tough and competitive, and climbing became the centre of their lives.

Pale-faced, long and lean, Arthur Dolphin was not from the same working-class background as most of the climbers emerging from Yorkshire's industrial towns. But, transcending social division, he had the universal respect of all. On the most testing of all gritstone outcrops, the overhanging Almscliff, he was the master, soloing with apparent ease, up and down, on the hardest routes of the day.

He opened his short campaign on the Scafells with a young and lithe Pete Greenwood. Their first route, Pegasus, was a rather wandering affair and they were forced to use aid on two of the pitches. But their next was quite different. Near the left side of the East Buttress hangs a huge and formidable corner, guarded by a short, vicious, overhanging crack – one of the most obvious and challenging lines to be found anywhere on Lakeland rock. Jim Birkett had tried it and backed off. On 24 May 1952, Greenwood and Dolphin climbed this route and named it Hell's Groove. Pete hand-jammed the crack, a technique perfected on his native gritstone outcrops, and Dolphin climbed the great corner above with a poor hand-inserted piton the only point of protection in virtually 30m of climbing. This sensational team effort proved that the next generation had arrived.

Dolphin's last route on the Scafells, Trespasser Groove, was climbed on 9 September 1952. Although flanking the central pillar, the great monolith that defines the crag, this was the best effort to date on the Esk Buttress, and there were to be no more. After making the first British ascent of a new route on the South Face of the Dent du Geant in the Chamonix Alps in July 1953, Dolphin slipped from the path on the descent and was killed.

A corner groove on the left side of the East Buttress was the next new climb of significance. Trinity, ascended on 5 June 1955, was a typical effort by Don Whillans – direct, straight and bold. With his slight height, razor-sharp wit, flat cap and laconic Lancashire accent, Whillans has attracted more tales and legends than any other climber I know. He rose from the back streets of Salford to become one of the greatest climbers on the world stage. Few have shown such mastery, ranging from cutting-edge routes on rock, including Peak gritstone and the mountain crags of

I offer no apologies; those who prefer to climb the place unaided are cordially invited to remove the piton and do so.

Significantly, it was another forty years before anyone did!

Even before the outbreak of World War II, a bitter twist of fate brought this fruitful period of development to a premature end. In 1934, high on the snow-plastered heights of Ben Nevis, Colin Kirkus, in the lead above Maurice Linnell, sustained a fall – perhaps due to an avalanche of unstable snow – which resulted in death for Linnell and serious injury for Kirkus. He never made a hard climb again, and died in the war. He left behind a wonderful legacy of

ABOVE: Jim Birkett, c. 1938.

ABOVE LEFT: Jim Birkett and Chuck Hudson on the first ascent of May Day Climb, East Buttress, 1 May 1938.

RIGHT: Climbers on the magnificent Hell's Groove, East Buttress, first ascended on 24 May 1952 by Pete Greenwood and Arthur Dolphin.

Wales, England and Scotland, to his mountaineering achievements in the Alps, South America and the Himalayas. There is probably a Don Whillans tale to match every climbing occasion. When someone once asked him how he reached the holds, being so short, he countered immediately with the retort: 'I climb to 'em.' This is what I tell my young son, should he ever struggle to reach a hold.

Near the end of the 1950s a number of major players pushed the limits on British rock, and a few of these tackled the East Buttress. Ron Moseley's Phoenix (1957) and Robin Smith's Chartreuse and Leverage (both 3 May 1958) were the best. Ron Moseley was one of the leading lights of the Rock and Ice, the now-legendary club for climbers based in the Manchester area, along with Don Whillans and Joe Brown; the year before, he had pioneered one of the most famous routes in North Wales, White Slab on Clogwyn Du'r Arddu. With a feast of groundbreaking routes in Scotland, in both summer and winter, and Alpine ascents of the highest calibre to his name, Robin Smith lost his life in the Russian High Pamirs. Looking at the legacy of his climbs, it is almost impossible to believe that he was only 23 when he died.

1960s: THE TIMES THEY ARE A-CHANGING

Climbing equipment and rope techniques were by now becoming significantly more sophisticated. A new type of climbing shoe known as the PA, with close-fitting canvas uppers and a rubber sole and rand, developed on the Fontainebleau boulders by Pierre Allain, had been imported from France by members of the Rock and Ice. Nylon climbing ropes were replacing hemp. Removable artificial nuts were being used for protection in addition to pitons hammered into the cracks.

Opening the decade on the East Buttress was Geoff Oliver's Ichabod, a touchstone route. Although some aid was used on the first ascent, when this was dispensed with it became *the* hard route to aspire to on the Scafells. Hot on its heels came the Centaur by gangly Les Brown. Climbed without aid (although pitons were used for protection), it tackled the central portion of the East Buttress. Brown had a discerning eye for quality lines and pioneered a host of tremendous and difficult routes throughout the Lake District. On 12 July 1966 he turned his attention to the slanting crack line left of the Central Buttress. He employed piton aid on the crack, but added a magnificent finish directly up the headwall, naming the route the Nazgul. The aided pitch was eventually free-climbed some ten years later.

These were edgy, competitive times with a number of individuals and groups vying to complete unclimbed lines. It is beyond the scope of this brief sketch to mention all those involved or the fine climbs they made, but perhaps one incident best illustrates the prevailing mood. The most obvious remaining challenge was the Central Pillar of Esk Buttress. It had already repulsed the greats from two previous generations, Jim Birkett in the 1940s and Arthur Dolphin in the 1950s. They had both flanked it, but the central face remained virgin.

Jack Soper abseiled down the buttress and discovered a line of weakness which he felt certain was possible to climb. He 'cleaned' off loose blocks and reported back to the bar of the Old Dungeon Ghyll Hotel that the route was ready to go. Unfortunately for the Lakeland locals, Welsh 'raiders', led by Pete Crewe, had overheard the animated conversations. Crewe made a dawn start and beat Allan Austin, Matey Metcalf and Soper to the route. On 17 June 1962, he claimed the first ascent of Lakeland's greatest unclimbed line, the Central Pillar of Esk Buttress. This was shades of Moss Ghyll some seventy years earlier! The deflated Lakeland lads settled for two flanking lines, the aptly named Black Sunday and the Red Edge. It was a bitter pill to swallow, but it must be said that the two compensatory routes were excellent climbs in their own right, particularly the Red Edge. In an unexpected way, the ascent of the latter had the most influence on what was to follow, because it so clearly showed that there was still much of quality to be found for those with the vision to seek it.

The last route of consequence in the 1960s really belongs to the next decade. Influential, innovative, long and demanding, potentially very serious, Lord of the Rings was climbed by Johnny Adams and Colin Read over two days on 14–15 June 1969. It offers some 365m of sustained and extremely difficult climbing, which traverses the full width of the East Buttress. A natural line of weakness with no easy escapes, this seemed like an Alpine challenge rather than a mere Lakeland rock climb. It did not receive a second ascent until a couple of up-and-coming challengers, myself and Ed Cleasby, climbed it in a single day in May 1975. Adams and Read were setting the Lakes alive at that time – the former with his perfection of technique and superb rope management, and the latter with his drive and eye for a line. I suspect no one can compare with Adams's sheer participation in rock climbing – he has climbed more rock worldwide than anyone I have ever known.

1970s: GLORY DAYS

Exciting and challenging times were emerging, with numbers of new quality routes and a cosmic increase in difficulty. A number of key factors propelled this period of Lakeland and Scafell climbing to the forefront of British rock climbing. Considerable advances in equipment contributed to a seismic change of attitude, and summers were long and dry. Strong, motivated teams were distributed throughout the region, many of them inspired by Ken Wilson's *Mountain Magazine* and his photographic book *Hard Rock*. And Pete Livesey – superstar, hero and villain – played a part.

People started the decade using a single hawser laid nylon rope tied around their waists, carrying heavy steel pegs and karabiners, with a peg hammer inevitably stuck in the back pocket. They belayed each other by running the rope around their backs and wrapping it around their wrists for security! Yet, in a very short space of time, climbers began to use two, infinitely superior, kernmantle ropes; wore comfortable harnesses (beginning with Don Whillans's revolutionary sit harness) which would absorb impact in the event of a fall; carried and used a huge variety of protection nuts that could be placed for security in either thin or large cracks, cams that expanded to fit different-sized cracks (called 'Friends' and designed by American aeronautical engineer Ray Jardine) and lightweight alloy karabiners, and belayed using specially designed belay plates which softened the load in the event of a fall. As the climbing became harder and more athletic, gymnasts' chalk was dusted on to the hands to improve grip. To cater for the rapidly increasing range of difficulty, Pete Botterill and the Carlisle lads developed a new, open-ended system of grading extreme climbs which became the British standard. To put it into some kind of context, the 1970s climbing gear evolution was akin to the difference between a 1960s Morris Minor and a 1970s Lotus Elan.

Right from the start of this period, the mindset had changed. Looking back, I think it was a lot to do with Adams's and Read's Lord of the Rings, employing only one solitary point of aid. This showed the way forward. News and images of the vertical world of California's Yosemite – sun-soaked naked granite, a rock climber's paradise – were also of considerable influence. On Scafell and throughout the Lakes, it became the thing to climb all the existing routes which had employed aid without it – that is, to climb them 'free'. As most aid points were dispensed with, pioneering new and harder routes became the primary objective.

When Chris Bonington and Nick Estcourt (who was to disappear on Everest) climbed White Wizard in 1971, a tremendous crack line running up the edge of the Central Buttress, they used six points of aid. Despite the fact that it was a fine and difficult route by two able climbers, they were out of sync with the mood of the time. A generation was looking anew at the ethics of climbing. Similarly, a route I pioneered in 1973 on the edge of Scafell Pinnacle, Edge Hog, I left for a whole year because I did not want to place a single piton on it, even though it would be for protection only and not aid. Even so, the old guard second-ascensionists placed a peg, believing it acceptable to do so. At the time this seemed to me a frustrating step in the wrong direction.

The conflict burst into the open and a line was drawn by the incomparable Pete Livesey. He had a string of brilliant and difficult routes to his name, including the two undisputedly hardest routes in Britain at the time: North Wales's Right Wall and Borrowdale's Footless Crow. He was a top-class athlete, one of a group of climbers to make their mark who had trained systematically on Leeds Wall, one of the earliest climbing walls in the country. He believed that all routes should be climbed free, without any artificial aid. It was acceptable to practise the route on a rope from above, or even to pre-place vital protection, so long as the actual ascent was done completely free.

On 5 May 1974, Rod Valentine and Tut Braithwaite alternated leads on one of the last great lines – an awesome overhanging and bottomless corner, straight up the face of the Central Pillar of the Esk Buttress. They used three points of aid on the Cumbrian, which they reported honestly. Both extremely powerful and talented climbers, if they had fully employed Livesey's ethics of pre-practice and anything-goes preparation prior to the ascent, they could doubtless have climbed it free straight off. But they didn't.

Livesey took up the pen in *Mountain Magazine* number 36:

Braithwaite and Valentine pulled the lowest trick in years. It was Valentine and his FRCC cronies who had a lot to say about leaving routes with aid out of the guide-books. 'Avoid the rush to get into print,' they said. 'If you can't do it without aid then leave it for someone better.' The various factions operating in the

Lakes couldn't help but agree with these strictures, so we all had a look at this Esk Buttress line and left it to someone better. The new guide was about to go into print and who rushed to get it in but Valentine and Tut. . . . I see the finished product, the route, as the important aspect of climbing new routes on British rock. It is perhaps better, therefore, to sacrifice some purity of approach in favour of leaving a clean, aid-free creation.

These words shook the old regime to the core, and set the tone for all that was to follow. It was an excellent piece of propaganda, but it should be said that using points of aid happened on a number of occasions and Livesey did not always follow his own high ideals. After making what was probably the second ascent of the Cumbrian, he claimed to have climbed it totally free. Unknown to him, however, unseen observers recorded that he used two points of aid! What was his reaction to being rumbled – mortification, guilt, repentance? Not a bit of it. Pete Livesey thrived on unconventionality and controversy; he believed all rules were for breaking – even his own.

Such was the proliferation of outstanding new routes that it is impossible to detail all that happened and everyone involved. Pete Livesey and Jill Lawrence climbed the great

Unquestionably the most prolific and productive of all who operated on the Scafells during these defining and glorious years were two of the talented Carlisle lads: gentle giant Jeff Lamb and, equally mild-mannered, the slight, though exceedingly powerful, Pete Botterill. The joke at the time was that Pete had gone to Yosemite as a climber of average performance and returned with the ability to climb harder than anyone else! Their achievements stretched to over a dozen exceedingly difficult routes, beginning and ending on the East Buttress with Zeus (1974) and finishing with the most difficult route of them all, appropriately named the Almighty (1981). Shortly after this, Jeff emigrated to Australia; he was found dead from head injuries in October 1983 in his car at the top of Frog Buttress, Queensland, where he had been climbing alone. It was the end of an era.

1980s: ADVENTURE CLIMBING

The pace of development now slowed dramatically. The Botterill and Lamb team was no more. Cleasby and Matheson climbed their last new route together in 1983, Shikasta on the East Buttress. With most of the then-obvious lines of weakness climbed, attention shifted away from the main crags of the Scafells. Other influences far away from these mountain crags, with their variable weather, weeping moss-filled cracks and lichened rocks, were also to play a major part.

With the advent on the Continent of 'sport climbing' – hard climbs protected by bolts, physically demanding but extremely safe – the popularity of the mountain routes fell away markedly. Many took to the new style of rock climbing on the limestone crags of Britain and Europe, though it was thought by the majority of British climbers to be unsuitable and unethical for British mountain crags; they called it 'the murder of the impossible'. The traditional type of British rock climbing, using natural cracks and features to place protection, became known as 'adventure climbing'.

A new trend was the development of the smaller crags that litter the flanks of the Massif. This was new rock for the taking, and it was relatively simple to practise and to clean the routes from a rope. The new ethic, 'red pointing', involved pulling the ropes down prior to making an accredited ascent; it was imperative to climb the route completely free and in good style, no matter what had gone before. Newly discovered crags in this category include Chamber's Crag, Spout Head Crag, Scar Lathing and Piers Gill Crag. Activists were many and included (in no particular order) Tom Walkington, Barry Rogers, Al Phizacklea, myself, Luke Steer, Paul Ross, Pete Greenwood (who had made the first ascent of Hell's Groove in 1952) and Ray McHaffie.

Of course, on the major crags there were a few exceptions to the general trend. My Antibody of 10 June 1984 on the Esk Buttress contained a short section of very hard technical and precarious climbing. Though the route of this decade was undoubtedly the magnificent and formidable Borderline on the East Buttress, climbed on 21 June 1986 with Chris Sowden and Martin Berzins alternating the lead, Siege Perilous was another of their extremely demanding pitches on the East Buttress. All these routes, though, were hybrids in a way; to a significant extent, they were climbed with the mindset that Pete Livesey's concept, of practising

open book overhanging corner of Lost Horizons on the East Buttress, one of the great lines. Afterwards, relaxing with other climbers on Mickledore, Livesey was asked by Pete Botterill if it had been free. Pete said it had. It was left to Jill to spill the beans with: 'What about that sling, Pete?' Livesey had pre-placed a long sling on a piton and used it to swing around the bulging top arête of the corner – so in fact it was not a free ascent!

The South Lakes team of Ed Cleasby and Rob Matheson (with a guest appearance by John Eastham) climbed four defining routes of the period. On the East Buttress, Cleasby finally won through on the overhanging Shere Khan with a point of aid, and Rob led the beautiful and bold Edge of Eriador. John Eastham, with a point of aid, led the sweeping wall right of Central Buttress's Great Flake to give the mighty Saxon. Andy Hyslop, Rick Graham and myself from the Central Lakes concentrated our efforts on the Esk Buttress, with the hanging arête of Fallout being the best of the bunch. Yorkshire raiders, brothers Martin and Bob Berzins, added Humdrum on the Esk Buttress and the powerful Cullinan on the East Buttress; Martin was also to accompany the next two climbers on a number of routes.

until perfect then making an immaculate ascent, was a little too radical. Mentally, those participating still had not made that significant psychological move.

On Antibody, although I was lowered down on a rope and climbed back out of the upper section, on the crux bottom section of the route I did not even inspect the holds, never mind practise until perfect. Aid was used on Siege Perilous, and on Borderline it took the combined efforts of both climbers before Chris finally won through. It was reported in *Mountain Magazine* Number 130 thus:

> Martin Berzins and Chris Sowden determinedly attacked the line with vigour, taking many falls, and as Martin revealed, 'We frigged it to death.'

But all was set to change.

1990s to 2000s: LONELY DAYS

Huge advances in sport climbing and in climbing walls have led to two differing approaches to rock climbing. For the majority, tempted by the security of bolt protection and the great crags of Europe, increased athleticism, strength, fitness and stamina have meant harder, more frequent sport climbing and bouldering. The Scafell crags are now noticeably quieter than in the 1960s or 1970s. For a minority who also have the mental control, commitment and boldness necessary for successful adventure rock climbing, the present level of climbing on the Scafells is probably, again, the hardest to be found in Britain.

One of the first routes of the new decade was really stunning, taking the blank impending wall left of the Cumbrian on the Esk Buttress. Dave Pegg's First Last and Always, climbed on 20 May 1990, fully embraced the lessons learnt by high-standard sport climbing and applied them to a mountain crag. On the East Buttress, Paul and Greg Cornforth took alternate leads on the Ambleside Brothers' Climb. A year later, Neil Foster added Desperately Sea King, named after an incident when a rescue helicopter's blade touched the crag mid-rescue and was forced to crash-land in the Great Moss below (see pages 28–29). On the left edge of the wall, left of the Cumbrian, Steve Crowe with Karen Magog cheekily slotted in the Northumbrian in 1994.

An event four years later heralded another new era on Scafell. Dave Birkett's ascent of New Horizons on 19 May 1998 was something else. Many had looked at the overhanging left arête of Lost Horizons, but all had dismissed it as too hard. Fully endorsing Livesey's philosophy that the actual ascent should be clean, with no points of aid, Birkett prepared for the route both mentally and physically before ascending it in immaculate style. It was probably the biggest leap in climbing standards since his grandfather, Jim Birkett, had made the first ascent of May Day Climb some sixty years earlier.

MORE ON SCAFELL AND THE BIRKETTS

Talking about one's own deeds goes against the instinct of Lakeland dales folk – it makes us feel uncomfortable and boastful, so we usually play down any achievements. Joss Naylor, fell-running legend from Wasdale, completed all 214 Wainwright Lakeland Peaks in a continuous run which took just under seven days, at the age of fifty. He wrote: 'I'm a man for doing, not saying,' and it is true that if you 'say nowt' it isn't easy to be misquoted. The alternative strategy is obvious exaggeration, as in the World's Biggest Liar competition held annually at Wasdale Head, in which the joke is ultimately on the questioner.

However, I am in a unique position to talk about the Birketts on Scafell, so I am going to add a little about what the mountain means to me, what I have done and what other Birketts have achieved. Within the context of the Lakeland Fells, Scafell is a relatively isolated massif. Its flora and fauna; its spectacular form; the ever-changing seasons, light and climatic conditions, and the rich history of man's involvement, particularly in climbing its great vertical cliff faces, are just some of the qualities that captivate me and the two other climbers in the family.

The name Birkett figures prominently in the history of climbing on Scafell, in the first recorded rock climb and also, as I write, in the last. The first was by Edward Birkett who, together with Jonathan Otley, climbed Broad Stand on 7 June 1815; the last, Return of the King, was made by Dave Birkett on 3 June 2006. Edward was aged 66 at the time, and had walked from Keswick to make the ascent; Dave is somewhat younger. Birkett is a fairly common Lakeland name with Viking origins, so we do not know for certain if Edward is related to our family, but we hope he is!

My father Jim Birkett was a quarryman from Little Langdale. A naturalist with a unique knowledge of mountain birds and flora, he has been described by many as the greatest rock climber of his generation. I am a climber too, and a writer and photographer specialising in the great outdoors and, naturally, my native Lakeland. Dave Birkett, a local stonemason, is my nephew, Jim's grandson, one of the finest adventure rock climbers in the world: he can turn up at just about any difficult climb and ascend it on sight.

Our routes have been at the cutting edge. Jim's May Day climb on the East Buttress in 1938 remained the hardest technical climb in the region until the 1960s. My Fallout on the Esk Buttress in June 1979 was one of the toughest routes of the 1970s. Dave currently has six desperate routes, all of which remain unrepeated – I won't be doing those, that's for sure: my role now when out with Dave is strictly photographer only! Birketts have contributed more to rock climbing on Scafell than any other single family.

So why all this involvement with a mountain? Undoubtedly it is something to do with the challenge on our home patch, but it is more than that. As Dave put it to me: 'It's just like a natural migration: when spring arrives you hear Scafell calling and you just have to get back up there.' The common thread between us is a love of mountains and Scafell in particular, and I cannot help but feel there is a strong spiritual element to it.

Jim Birkett was a hard man – uncompromising, intelligent and principled. A quarryman of enormous physical strength, he was a 'river' who split slate with a hammer and chisel. He loved poetry, plants and birds, and he lived for the mountains. He climbed with a minimum of equipment in the days when climbing was a much more dangerous game: the lead climber could not afford to make a slip or take a fall. His reputation was of fearlessness and of putting up climbs previously thought impossible. He dominated the scene for a decade, then stopped, and said very little more about it. That was it; he'd done it. Mountains and wild places, their bird life and flora and fauna, remained very much on his agenda. During the great pesticide scare of the 1960s, when the peregrine falcon almost became extinct in Britain, he was one of the few people granted a licence by the Nature Conservancy Council to visit the nests of birds of prey to mark their eggs to make them valueless to collectors. Weekends and holidays, even early mornings and evenings outside his day's work, we were always out on the mountains together. I took my first photographs then, of birds' eggs and chicks, often as not lowered on a rope to the nest by Jim.

Another influence on my view of the mountain habitat was Derek Ratcliffe, Chief Scientist to the Nature Conservancy Council and a great friend of my father. With his breathtaking knowledge of life within the natural world and his command of mountain terrain, he exuded quiet power and a sense of natural order. As a youngster, following these two men of the mountains to observe the site of an eagle or to search for a particular fern was a thrilling experience for me. Best of all were Derek's remarkable photographic slide-shows, staged for our benefit.

My earliest recollection of Scafell is visiting Cam Spout, the steep, broken and richly vegetated crag overlooking Great Moss. Home to the peregrine falcon and the raven, it was a favourite springtime crag on Jim Birkett's itinerary. Mostly we followed the track up Mosedale, descending to Lingcove Beck, then leaving the regular paths to take a route beneath Long Crag on what Jim called the 'Falconer's Path'. Looking across the wildness of Great Moss to the full might of the Scafells left an indelible mark on me; it is still one of my favourite mountain places and I always thrill to the view of the great pillar of naked rock that is Esk Buttress.

I made my first real rock climb on Scafell, with two schoolfriends, when I was about fifteen. We arrived with our tent and all the equipment after struggling along the Corridor Route from Styhead via Seathwaite in Borrowdale. It was a glorious evening, so we dumped our gear opposite the East Buttress and immediately climbed the magnificent classic of Great Eastern. It was one of those magical moments, the memory of which stays with you for life. It just seemed so easy, like a stroll in the park – we felt as if there wasn't a route we couldn't climb, we could do anything. The innocence of youth!

During the night, a stream began to flow through our tent and we woke to a scene of wind, swirling cloud and driving rain. And that is how it stayed for the next two days, after which we staggered down to Wasdale Head, cold, soaking and just a little dispirited. Worse was to come. On that first evening, a group of children with special needs had walked past our encampment, descending to Great Moss and presumably down to Eskdale. One lagging behind the rest, obviously suffering, had stopped to chat with us before continuing his awkward and painful progress down. At Wasdale Head we learned that, separated from the rest of his group, he had died from exposure. This was our welcome to the cruel world and our first hard lesson of the mountains.

My new routing activities on the Scafells commenced in 1972, peaked around a decade later and spluttered to a close later in the 1980s. There were many moments of earnest intent, but chiefly it was a time of fun and laughter. One route I was particularly happy to have climbed was the arête of Fallout on Esk Buttress. This was by default, since it was Andy Hyslop's line. He had identified its possibilities and I was merely enlisted to hold the ropes and provide moral support. Andy was a very competent and ambitious young climber who, like all of us, wanted to make a big impression. His chief virtue was daring: he was very cool and composed on the big lead and nothing seemed to throw him out. In attempting to reach the hanging arête he had a number of falls, with me holding him on the rope. This was before the belay plate had become widely accepted and I was simply holding him with the rope running around my back and wrapped around my bare wrists. On his last fall, I was twisted upside-down and smashed into the belay, with the smell of burning flesh from my hands and wrists sharp in my nostrils. At this point I had to concede that the advice of Rick Graham, my frequent climbing partner – that to climb without a belay plate was nothing short of irresponsible – was sound. Naturally enough, Andy wanted to pack it in after that. But inexplicably, as though some primeval energy had been activated, I felt determined we should do it, and went on to lead it.

Dave Birkett did not start climbing until his early twenties, which counts as a late start. He spent much of his early life farming the high fells around Great Langdale, and had a strong affinity with the hills from an early age. As a schoolboy he was a champion fell runner, a proper athlete. He started climbing with Tom Walkington and Barry Rogers, two old climbing friends of mine, who urged him to knock on my door to see if I would take him out.

A few months later we got together to make the fiftieth anniversary ascent of Jim Birkett's great route, Overhanging Bastion, on the Castle Rock of Triermain. Dave still says that I charged him petrol money and led the best pitch! Maybe so, but afterwards I pointed him up a much harder route, known as Ted Cheasby, which he climbed, if not with ease, then certainly with huge energy and determination. It was immediately obvious to me that Dave had that fluidity of movement, that intelligence on rock, which you cannot learn. I smiled inwardly in the knowledge that here was a very bright star rising.

In quick succession Dave accompanied me on a number of climbing trips around Britain and France. Very soon he was climbing routes I could not follow, and had the temperament to laugh gently at my frustrations. What immediately struck me about Dave was not only his obvious love and enthusiasm for climbing, at which he is simply a genius, but his fascination with the natural world and life in general. We had marvellous days together, and I felt as privileged to be with him as I had felt on the mountains with my father many years before.

Soon he was gone with a young, keen set of climbers who were to make their name in the Lakes. Dave's string of mind-blowingly difficult new climbs on Scafell, particularly those on the East Buttress, outrank all that has gone before. The lines he climbed, beginning in 1998 with Talbot Horizons and (at the time of writing) ending with Return of the King in 2006, are almost unbelievable. They are not merely hard variations of existing routes, but the glaring challenge of

RIGHT: Dave Birkett cuts loose
on one of his East Buttress
routes: the overhanging arête
of Talbot Horizons, first climbed
on 28 July 2000.

hanging arêtes, searing cracks and huge blank walls that others have thought impossible. Like Jim Birkett before him, he has dazzled the climbing world and it is difficult to see how his achievements on Scafell could ever be equalled.

Two years after his historic New Horizons, on 28 July 2000 he ascended the even harder Talbot Horizons, the right arête of Lost Horizons. This involved a totally committing sequence of crux moves from which a fall would most likely have proved fatal. Technically, his hardest ascent to date came with Welcome to the Cruel World, climbed on 19 April 2002, involving dynamic moves to tiny finger pockets. A full-page photograph of his ascent was printed in the prestigious French magazine *Vertical*; it felt as if Scafell was again in the mainstream of world climbing. Another Lonely Day followed the same spring, and since then Dave has added two more routes. A prizewinning film about Dave, *Set in Stone: Profile of a Lakeland Rock Climber*, made in 2006 (available on DVD), includes breathtaking footage of his first ascent of Return of the King.

At the time of writing, not one of Dave's routes has had a second ascent. Like the greats of yesteryear – Jones, Botterill and Herford – Dave Birkett is out there on his own,

head and shoulders above the rest. Some may put his success down to his pedigree, but I don't think that has much to do with it. Long, lean, with an exceptional physique, Dave has always been an outstanding athlete. And since he began climbing he has made it, and Scafell, the centre of his life.

Throughout this historic period I was able to capture the action in photography. It was an exciting time, and to have been in a position to illustrate the beauty and drama of Dave's climbing has been tremendously satisfying. To portray the magic and power of the Scafells, to touch the spirit of the mountain through my imagery, is something for which I am immensely grateful. I feel Jim Birkett would have been proud of us both.

POSTSCRIPT

As I write this, it is hard to see where the future of climbing lies on the Scafells, since there is not a great deal of unclimbed rock left. But each generation has thought that, and each has been proved wrong, as I am sure I will be. In a way it isn't important. To get out on the peerless crags of Scafell, do your own thing and enjoy it is all that really matters.

BELOW: The East Buttress of Scafell, bathed in spring sunshine. On this occasion, after setting up camp, we climbed the magnificent Great Eastern route, which tackles the very centre of the crag. Surely, nothing could stop our progress. The next morning, however, our tent flooded, and in the rain and heavy cloud we could not even see the East Buttress. Take opportunities while you can and never bank on fine weather in the mountains!

INDEX

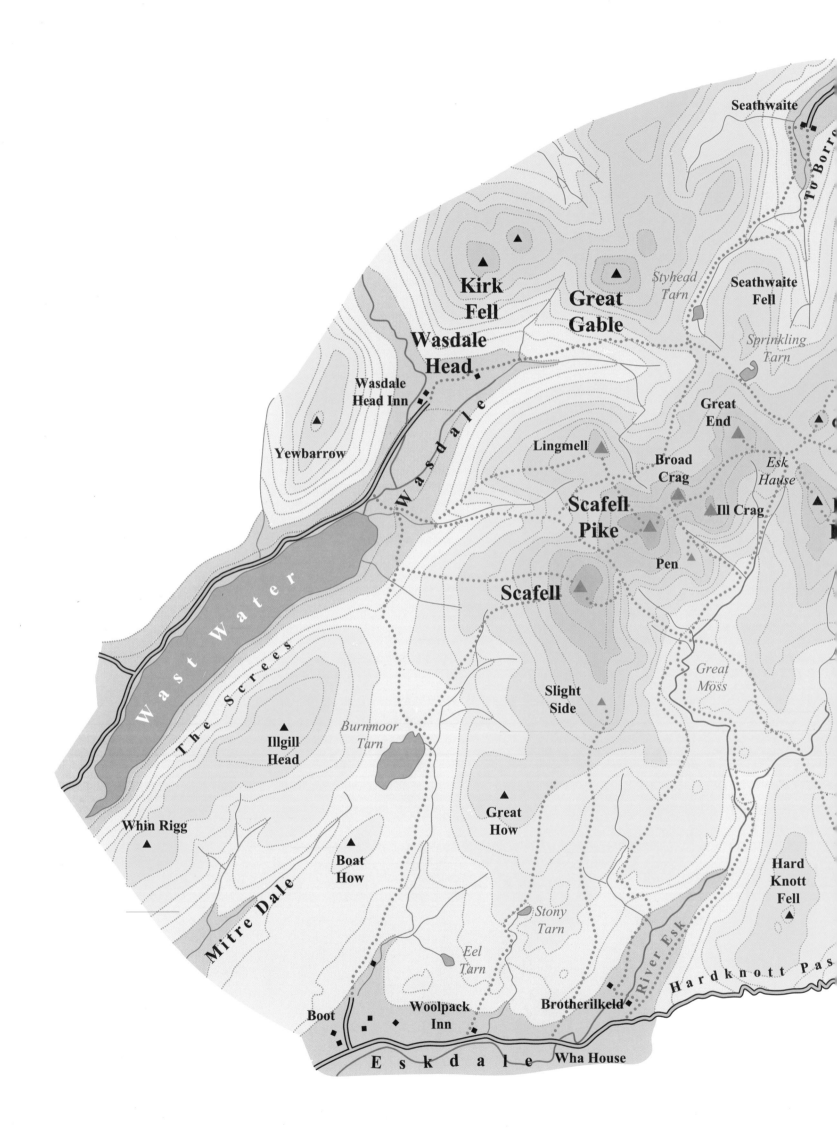

Seathwaite

To Borro

Kirk
Fell

Great
Gable

Styhead
Tarn

Seathwaite
Fell

Wasdale
Head

Sprinkling
Tarn

Wasdale
Head Inn

Great
End

Lingmell

Broad
Crag

Esk
Hause

Yewbarrow

Scafell
Pike

Ill Crag

Pen

Scafell

Wast Water

Great
Moss

Slight
Side

The Screes

Burnmoor
Tarn

Illgill
Head

Whin Rigg

Great
How

Hard
Knott
Fell

Boat
How

Mitre Dale

Stony
Tarn

River Esk

Hardknott Pas

Eel
Tarn

Boot

Woolpack
Inn

Brotherilkeld

Eskdale

Wha House